MORE THAN NINE LIVES WITH
GOD

BY JOHN COLEMAN

Copyright © 2015 by John Coleman

MORE THAN NINE LIVES WITH GOD
by John Coleman

Rev. ed.

ISBN 9780645582505

All rights reserved solely by the author. The author guarantees all contents are original and do not infringe upon the legal rights of any other person or work. No part of this book may be reproduced in any form without the permission of the author. The views expressed in this book are not necessarily those of the publisher.

Unless otherwise indicated, Scripture quotations are taken from the New International Version (NIV). Copyright © 1973, 1978, 1984, 2011 by Biblica, Inc.™. Used by permission. All rights reserved.

Dedication

I dedicate this book to Norma, Bettina, Jonathan, and Glen, as well as other family members and friends, and to those trying to find meaning, fulfilment, purpose, and answers to their difficulties and hearts' desires, especially in finding **God, faith,** success, true joy, and peace of mind.

Acknowledgements

I would like to thank my sister, Catherine, for checking the accuracy of notable facts about my life and for checking some of my work. Catherine is a talented teacher and the author of many children's books, including one about native plants for a well-known photographer. I would also like to thank her husband, Terry, and my sister, Diana, for their encouraging comments. In addition, I would like to thank my wife, Norma, and my children, Jonathan, Glen, and Bettina, for their encouragement and help. Additionally, I would like to thank those in our church who know me and are a blessing and our connect group for their prayers, encouragement, and support, including those who checked through this book and gave valuable help and advice, and especially God for His spiritual guidance in the preparation of this book.

Table of Contents

Introduction xi

Chapter 1   My Mother 17

Chapter 2   My Father's Narrow Escapes
            During the War 21

Chapter 3   Mariri in New Zealand 33

Chapter 4   Amberley in New Zealand 41

Chapter 5   Holidays in New South Wales, Australia 49

Chapter 6   Our Move to Melbourne in Australia 49

Chapter 7   Teenage Years 59

Chapter 8   Change Around the World. 83

Chapter 9   A Trip to New Zealand 95

Chapter 10 Four Years in New South Wales 99

Chapter 11 Our Trip to Darwin 107

Chapter 12 Back to Melbourne to Live 111

Chapter 13 A Miracle Occurs 117

Chapter 14 My Nursery Business 125

Chapter 15	Visit to the Philippines	129
Chapter 16	Single Again	137
Chapter 17	I Marry Again	143
Chapter 18	A Disastrous Fishing Trip	145
Chapter 19	Our Children	151
Chapter 20	In the Right Place to Help Others	155
Chapter 21	Some Dangerous Journeys	159
Chapter 22	Our Move to Macleay Island	163
Chapter 23	Looking to God Again for Healing	169
Chapter 24	Life on the Island	179
Chapter 25	Life on the Mainland	195
Chapter 26	Conclusion	205
Endnote		219

Introduction

This exciting and remarkable, yet nevertheless true, life story is about how God miraculously saved me so many times from losing my life. He also gave me a miraculous infilling of the Holy Spirit, followed by the experience of His extraordinarily powerful, unconditional love and astonishing events that followed this infilling. Apart from being, to a degree, an autobiography, most importantly it tells how God worked so miraculously. The trials faced in life eventually led me to rely on God, with the realisation that I could not do it alone. When learning and growing in faith, He proved Himself to be genuine and a most wonderful help to change my life for the better, especially when putting Him before everything else.

Not long ago, I realised that writing about the trials and escapes from death could be a witness to God's unconditional love and that He had saved me so that the truth could be told to help your faith; that you might come to Him and find Him genuine. Also, the extraordinary infilling of the Holy Spirit that followed convinced me totally of His reality. Telling you about this miracle and His saving power is the principal reason for writing this book, which you will find captivating and which will help improve your life for the better. I will mention verses from the Bible throughout my book to support my experiences to help you, as Christians consider them very reliable advice, and the Word of God, as they have withstood much analysis and the test of time. In **Psalm 23:4 (NIV), it says,** *"Even though I walk through the valley of the shadow of death, I will fear no evil, for you are with me; your rod and your staff, they comfort me."* The Lord can protect us from dangers and difficulties in life, so we can show confidence or faith in His power to help and protect us, just as David did here in the psalms. Coming to know God and trusting in Him will surely change our lives. My desire is that whoever reads this true story will find God, who desires to help us all and bring true joy and peace. Although my journey in life was difficult at times, it was worth it if this book helps you.

Experiencing God's unconditional love was such an incredible and exciting experience that the world just had to know. Reading recently of a woman's explanation of having similar spiritual experiences as me, but much later in 2010, left me astounded, thus confirming even more so that it must have been God giving us these amazing infilling touches (See Scarlett2, 2011).

Like I did, many people throughout the world having difficult lives or severe losses finally realised the need to rely on God and Christ Jesus for help and have had their lives turned around and changed into blessings far beyond their expectations. I realise God is using me as a messenger to pass on the Good News about His great love and desire to help us, if we would only realise it. It

Introduction

is truly sad to see people going through life, not realising or not believing this truth—suffering and dying without knowing Christ Jesus and God and missing the blessings they could have had.

A brief but true history of my life is written for you to show the reality of our loving God, principally because of the many times my life was nearly lost—near-death experiences you might say—through no fault of mine, but for some reason, being saved extraordinarily through divine intervention.

As mentioned, survival would have been impossible without some powerful spiritual intervention, and why should He bother with me? I felt that I was just an average person, yet maybe this is just the point—to show that God cares very much for all people and can use anybody as a vessel to show His loving power in many different ways. A person's achievements can be an inspiration to others, in helping others or in bringing others to the Lord. Everybody has talents; this is due only to His power whether people realize this or not, just as He shows in the Bible with Paul, who, although being special in God's sight, He kept him humble and in need of Him in order to achieve much for humanity.

Some stories need mentioning for accuracy, including illnesses that beset me that I would prefer not to mention, but I know that I need to so that others will understand how genuine and wonderful the Lord is. There are also some funny tales, as my life was not all emergencies. These just need mentioning to show Gods saving power.

I hope that one may learn and grow, in order to help others and glorify His Holy name. However, I have made an effort to tell this life story with humility, for without God, I cannot do anything, so the glory is His. I was one who liked to go hunting and fishing and made mistakes, like anybody else. After the amazing Holy Spirit infilling, I preferred not to hunt anymore but rather just take photos of God's wonderful creations instead.

Later in life, when afflicted with an illness called Chronic Fatigue Syndrome (CFS) and Post-traumatic Stress Disorder (PTSD), in my attempt to resolve these ailments, the resultant frustration led me to believe in and rely on God even more. In my need, through prayer, He showed His existence and help in many ways, just as He did with Paul in the Bible. See **2 Corinthians 12:10 (NIV)**: *"That's why, for Christ's sake, I delight in weaknesses, in insults, in hardships, in persecutions, in difficulties. For when I am weak, then I am strong."* Through the Holy Spirit, Paul gained spiritual strength, and through his weaknesses, he had to rely on God for His power to help humanity. He realized that the glory was not his, but God's. This was a very important lesson humanity needed to learn.

I have often wondered about, but only realised in the past few years, the reason for these troubles and realised why now, like Paul—so I can testify to the loving nature of our God. He is here to help us all, to guide us, and to help us through life, and we can reach out to Him through sincere seeking in prayer.

So in this story, I do not look for sympathy, pity, neither complaining, neither bragging, nor making excuses about what happened to me, only having to mention certain experiences so that one will eventually see the reality and amazing power of God in

Introduction

action, *for it is not about me; instead, it is about the wonderful caring, saving, and healing power of God, and to Him the glory is due.* I am no longer ashamed to testify to the truth of reliance upon, and knowing God, as it really is so important. I was not a little angel either, far from perfect, yet God is using me now to help people; however, I do not wish to preach. I only try to explain spiritual matters relative to my own experience to help with an understanding of the reasoning behind some of the incredible experiences I had and can only offer one main explanation for them—God's intervention. I feel, however, I should mention some scriptures to support some of my deep convictions and beliefs, which I sincerely believe are very important for all humanity to know about. I feel the Lord would be very disappointed if I left them out.

Through my experiences in life, the Holy Spirit has compelled me to tell these true stories to show that God and the spiritual world are genuine, and I feel you will find these stories astounding. Sometimes I may refer to God as the Father, at other times Jesus the Son of God, and at other times the Holy Spirit. However, as you may already know, the Christian Church calls this the Trinity, consisting of the Father, the Son, and the Holy Spirit.

There are many things to discuss; however, I must try to keep to the relevance of my experience. Being out sometimes in the bush with nature had its blessings because it was, in a way, finding God for me, finding time to relax amongst his creations, meditating on nature's beauty and thus tuning into God even more so. Read **Job 12:7–10 (NIV) and Psalm 24:1 (NIV).** God uses the Earth to teach us. Some stories are exciting, and some are funny like a good movie but should not disturb you. *Firstly, mentioning a brief history about my mother and father is important, as it will show you how God saved them also during dangerous times in their lives, and their stories are truly astounding. Although I have mentioned my father's war history in some detail, it is not to glorify war but to show the courage, suffering, sacrifices, and risks that many of our men put themselves under, as Jesus had done for us, so that we may all live in peace and security as we are meant to. It is important to be grateful for what they had done and to remember them, just as it is to remember Jesus, who suffered and was the greatest sacrifice of all time for us. Read on, and become amazed by what God has done and what He can do for you.*

Chapter 1

My Mother

Before the Second World War my parents met in New Zealand at an army dance, as my mother was on holiday from Australia. She grew up on a wheat and sheep farm in the outback of New South Wales, the family having originally come from Salisbury in South Australia. My sister Catherine discovered recently that our mother's original ancestors had arrived by sailing ship in the Nelson region in New Zealand, where we lived as children, but they decided to return to Adelaide in Australia because of the fighting going on around the Nelson district between the Maoris and whites. One of these ancestors served in Parliament in Adelaide before they moved to Salisbury.

Eventually my mother's parents, Stanley and Mabel, moved to the Forbes area of New South Wales and took up farming. My mother, Evelyn, had two sisters and two brothers. When she was seventeen, she rode a horse eight miles to teach Sunday school and was a wonderful Christian. She drove wheat trucks and rode a motorbike helping on the farm, so she was quite versatile. She helped look after her younger brother David when her father died. When the war was looming, she studied nursing and became an ambulance driver in Sydney, picking up from the ships wounded soldiers that had been fighting in Papua New Guinea and the Pacific Islands. There was such a concern about attack in Sydney that all lights had to be out when picking up wounded soldiers from the ships. A submarine attack eventually occurred, which sank a ferry in the harbour. Some soldiers, whom she cared for, became lifelong friends. She received the British and Australian service medals, awarded only after she had passed away.

She was a devout Christian all her life and gave her all to help people—she was selfless, humble, and a remarkable and special person. Mum's mother, Mabel, wrote this in a letter to Dad's mother in New Zealand when she met Dad in Sydney near the time of my parent's wedding. *"I do hope you will grow to love my little girl. She has always been like sunshine to me, and if she is just half as good a wife to Douglas as she has been daughter to me you will be satisfied with her."*

After locating one of her old school friends in a Brisbane home a few years ago, when mentioning to her that Evelyn was my mother, she nearly collapsed with delight. She told me that my mother was her fondest friend and the loveliest person she had ever known. She mentioned some experiences in life, the sense of humour, and the pleasant, remarkable spirit that my mother had.

For example, once she pinned a notice on the back of one of her teachers—how daring. Remembering her as a caring and loving person, one could feel her loving nature as she brushed our hair as children. When she became terminally ill, we tried in many ways to help her, including taking her to a healing meeting, as she had a brain tumour and could not speak.

She was also a clever poet, writing wonderful poetry and winning prizes when young, and she loved the Australian bush and painting landscapes, in which she would sometimes incorporate people, family, and friends. She loved playing the piano and having sing-songs with us as we grew up, especially Christian music. She also loved children, especially caring for my daughter Bettina as a baby after my first wife died, and teaching Sunday school. She was spiritual and close to God, having remarkable wisdom. Her tombstone bears the words *"A very special person"*.

Chapter 2

My Father's Narrow Escapes During The War

Being a New Zealander, my father, Douglas, grew up on a farm in Canterbury, his grandparents being some of the first settlers in this area. The original families came out from Ireland and Scotland on sailing ships. One of these stopped off at Melbourne on the way to New Zealand. At the time, a gold rush was well under way in Victoria, so everybody abandoned ship to try their luck on the goldfields. Another three months at least passed before they finally left for New Zealand in the 1850s. They took up farming back in the hills many miles from the nearest town, so they had to learn to be tough in those days. Dad told of our great-grandmother having to ride a horse over the hills and across fast-flowing riverbeds to give birth to a child in Christchurch.

My great-grandfather Sam married Catherine and had many children. One of the children, called Fred, my grandfather, had many sisters, our Aunts, who provided a stop-off and rest spot for travellers called "Riverside", and this old homestead has many happy memories.

My father went to college in Christchurch, where he became proficient in agricultural speaking competitions, often winning. He had to leave school early after his father died in 1933 to run the farm with his brother Ross. He continued to run the farm until 1939 when it became necessary for him to join the 2nd New Zealand Division, as the Second World War was impending, so his brothers Ken and Philip, nice chaps, ran the farm to support their mother.

Dad's sister June, a wonderful, and inspiring person, was a schoolteacher when younger. Dad wrote many letters to my mother Evelyn, as well as his mother Catherine, and June, during the war, and it was thoughtful of them to keep these letters and photographs. My thoughtful kind sister Catherine, having great fortitude, after major knee operations, put these letters and photos together with my father producing a remarkable book calling it, *When the Wisteria Blooms*. Only forty copies of these were made for family members. As Dad said from the war front, he would be home when the wisteria bloomed. Fortunately, this book was just finished before he died, so it was a wonderful tribute for him.

Dad went to train at the Burnham military barracks near Christchurch, and he was to train in the Canterbury Yeomanry Cavalry. The later use of Dad's old saddle rug from those times was on a horse we purchased. Dad and Mum became fond of each other after meeting at an army dance; they exchanged photographs and wrote to each other regularly while Dad was away at the war.

After leaving their cherished families, wives, and girlfriends, the Maori farewell, *"Now is the hour"*, rang out to them. Can you imagine the emotions they must have all been feeling? Thousands of men would never come home again, leaving many poor mothers with the loss of their sons. They set off from New Zealand on large, sophisticated passenger liners adorned with swimming pools. They were proud and bold, thinking they would whip the hides of these peace-breakers, but they found this more difficult than they could imagine. This would be the last time many would feel luxury before the difficulties ahead.

Each ship held thousands of troops. Dad had the duty of checking all the mail on board for any information that could jeopardize the safety of the ship and military plans. When they arrived in Cairo and Alexandria, they had to continue training, with Dad leading marching teams of soldiers. They managed to find time to climb the pyramids and see some Egyptian relics, buildings, and tombs.

My father was one of the officers in charge of the Tutankhamen treasures, ancient Egyptian gold and treasures worth countless millions. These treasures were removed from the museum in Cairo and placed back in old tombs under heavy guard, as Rommel was on the move towards Alexandria after defeating the British 8th Army along the North African coast.

Dad had so many astonishing stories and sometimes worked with the army Chaplain, so he had his own quiet faith. When they had made it compulsory for the men to go to a Sunday service while in Africa, many men did not turn up, so they were surprised that when they made it non-compulsory, more men came along; reverse psychology perhaps.

During the six years of service, he was involved in many major battles. Dad was involved in transporting troops, equipment, and supplies to battle areas and building up a large supply dump, thousands of gallons of fuel, and water for the Americans and Allies in the North African desert. They also had the responsibility of helping with the rounding up of hundreds of thousands of surrendered Italian prisoners and the enormous task of keeping water and food supplied to them.

A large Australian and New Zealand task force had diverted from North Africa to defend Greece against the German invasion; my father was one of those sent. This was difficult as the German Panzer divisions had large supplies of tanks, and the New Zealanders, Australians, and Greek army only had principally infantry, with little heavy artillery and inferior air support, which eventually could not hold out against the more powerful German offences.

In the mountains of Greece, they had to blow up bridges behind them to slow the German advance, and this was the time Dad had two German bombs fall on either side of him, covering him with mud—*neither of them exploding*—a miracle as this is a one in a million chance. Richard, a friend, told me recently that because of sabotage in the bomb factories of Germany, some workers deliberately avoided putting detonators in the bombs, so Dad had them, and God, to thank.

On the retreat, one of Dad's trucks had broken down when they were heading south for an eventual evacuation to Crete, and Dad went back with a mechanic to rescue it. On the way back, the Germans had broken through and put up a machinegun post. When Dad and the mechanic arrived, the Germans said, "Halt", pointing guns at them. Best not to say what the driver said back to the Germans before putting his foot flat on the accelerator, level with the gravel; he drove through the post with a liberal sprinkling of language, followed by a hail of bullets, but luckily they escaped.

They reached the coast eventually but had to leave all their trucks and equipment behind. They were crammed on rescue ships with only their rifles. Their next port of call was Crete, the defence of which was crucial to stopping the Germans from achieving their goals. The Allies built defences around the island, which turned out to be of no help whatsoever, and another mistake was leaving the airfields open. Holding the airfields on Crete was critical, but the determination of the Germans in sending in Para troops and forced aircraft landings on the airstrips eventually gained them the upper hand. Many tens of thousands of Australian, New Zealander, British, Cretan, Greek, and German troops died in this invasion, and my father told me this was the most desperate, intense, and nasty fighting in which he had ever been involved. He said they found stimulant drugs on some of the Germans, perhaps to give themselves a fighting edge.

The Maori Battalions of New Zealand were highly regarded for their efforts, especially in trying to regain the airfields under intense machinegun fire, as well as in acting as a rear-guard for the Allies' retreat over the mountains. Their determination and fighting spirit during the war made the enemy fear them, as the Maoris would put chase, shouting their Haka war cries, thus deserving much respect for their efforts. Some looked on the Germans as the baddies at the time; however, they were people like us, sadly led by a misguided leader under the power of the evil one, with strong Nazi authorities under him, whom it was at their peril to disobey.

In a few battles, some of Dad's men died next to him. It was a normal reaction when many cried for their mothers when they died, not only in Crete but also in the assault on the monastery of Monte Casino in Italy. The Germans were using it as a fortress, with heavy artillery weapons to slow the advance of American and Allied troops. The loss of close friends like this was a sad, deeply hurtful, and angering experience for most soldiers in battle. As a leader, my father had to make fast snap decisions to save their lives, and given only two choices, one had to choose the better of two evils; these were some of the difficulties of war. However, he did not have time to brood over these things, as officers had to keep themselves alert and under control for the continuing safety of their men and success in their campaigns.

Only having a pistol at hand, Dad had another encounter with a German armed with a machine gun, where Dad's cunning actions saved his own life. Dad had so many escapes from death himself—from machinegun bullets in Crete to aircraft bullets in

Greece passing through his truck and coming to rest in a can of bully beef right behind his back. In addition, the unexploded bombs falling next to him, as previously mentioned. At one stage, he was wounded with shrapnel and had many gunfights with Germans, including nasty experiences I would not want to depress you with, where God saved him just in time.

Once the Germans secured the airfields in Crete, General Freyberg, the New Zealand leader, with other generals, decided they had to retreat over the mountains of Crete; food being scarce, a friend of Dads pulled out the only biscuit he had in his pocket, but it was stuck to a cake of soap, so he would have been foaming at the mouth, anyway only a few thousand men boarded the ships, principally officers, including my father and Captain Charles Upham, who was awarded two Victoria Crosses. Major General Kippenberger said to King George VI, "In my respectful opinion Sir, Upham won the VC several times over". Charles Upham's war history story of his bravery is truly remarkable. As there were, too many men ashore to go aboard the ships, those left, including New Zealanders, Australians, and British troops, were imprisoned.

Dad was lucky enough to board an Australian frigate, called the *"Nizam"*, and soon after departure, German bombs lifted its stern completely out of the water. The men had to manhandle all the shells to the guns after the bombs disabled the ship's hydraulics. Many years later, when in hospital after a car accident, Dad discovered that the fellow in the bed next to him had been an engineer on that same ship at the same time—what a small world.

Back in North Africa, more battles continued, but at one stage when things were quieter, Dad, and teams of men went to Syria near Turkey for training manoeuvres, as read in one of Dad's letters. After being there for only a short time, they had to race back 1,500 miles to Matruh, where they had to take up defences against Rommel again on his advance towards Cairo.

At a later stage when the Germans were retreating, the Americans needed supplies taken over the mountains in Tunisia to help cut off Rommel's Army on his retreat. The mountains were too rugged for the trucks, so they asked Dad, being a farmer, to form a mule pack company to carry supplies over the mountains. He visited Arab communities, and after some hassles, he gathered together 101 mules and 96 donkeys, and training for this venture began. The New Zealand Army treats this as a special episode of their history and had a statue made of the soldiers and mules of which my father was in charge. They called this the 1 NZ Mule Pack Company Tunisia. (*See Victoria University of Wellington, 2014*, entry in Bibliography, for a reference to some of the campaigns my father, Major D.F. Coleman OBE, was in during the war.)

After this, Dad went on to Italy, and his brothers, Ken and Philip, wanted to join the war effort, but my father told them it was nasty, and there was no joy in it; however, Philip arrived soon after. They landed in Southern Italy and slowly regained territory from the Germans and eventually Rome itself, where they were warmly welcomed. Later they had to do more fighting up in the snow-covered mountains of Northern Italy.

Later in life, when I was working for the CSIRO in irrigation research with an Italian fellow who came from Northern Italy, he said the Germans rounded him up and sent him to Germany to work on locomotives, which Allied bombs and artillery had damaged.

Many troops sailed back from the North African front to defend Australia and New Zealand from a possible Japanese invasion, but Dad had to stay on, so it was only after many years away that he finally returned to New Zealand; however, this was not the end of dramas for him.

When approaching Australia in the Indian Ocean in one of two twin sister ships, one was attacked and sunk by a Japanese submarine, so the surviving ship, which Dad was on, headed rapidly towards Antarctica to escape. He finally arrived in Melbourne and went to Sydney by train, where he married my mother. They then flew back to New Zealand with other officials in one of Winston Churchill's planes, fitted with luxurious furniture. When crossing the Tasman Ocean, one of the engines cut out; however, they just managed to land in Christchurch safely. Soon after the flight, the plane disappeared, as it was lost at sea. Mum and Dad were certainly fortunate that the plane managed to land safely and that they were not on that last fatal flight. *God saved them again.*

After serving well as a captain in the 4th RMT Transport Company, Dad was promoted to Major, being highly commended for his service, and awarded nine medals, including the "Order of the British Empire", OBE. Henderson mentioned him in many dispatches in the book called *RMT: Official History of the 4th and 6th Reserve Mechanical Transport Companies, 2 NZEF:* (1954).

The Index URL gives a list of all pages in the above book where Henderson mentions my father's (D.F. Coleman) dispatches, plus a photo and other references are shown on the other URL in the Bibliography, as quoted above from the Victoria University of Wellington, 2014.

Dad was humble, not taking credit for this honour, and said in his letters that the honour went to his men, just as Charles Upham the war hero said of himself in his book, *Mark of the Lion*.

Settling back into civilian life was difficult for my father, as it was for many other soldiers, especially those with post-traumatic stress from war activities, called "shell shock", which was not fully recognized or understood at the time. Counselling to soldiers was not even considered as it is today, and many soldiers were mentally distraught from the traumas of war and had little help or understanding. This affected and ruined many marriages.

My father went back to the Victory Parade in London, leading his troops in the march, and he was one of a few New Zealanders privileged to be invited to Hampton Court Palace, where he spoke personally to the King, Queen, and Queen Mary for several minutes. He stayed with his older brother Ross and his wife Connie. Ross was a wireless operator on a ship and escaped death himself after the enemy torpedoed the ship.

Although Dad and Mum were fortunate in coming through the war and seemed okay most of the time, the number of traumas and war experiences they had seen most likely could have caused some trauma. Trying to put such things behind them and going ahead positively into the future must have been difficult. I wonder, though, how much they suffered emotionally. Nevertheless, for most of my life, Mum and Dad seemed positive, perhaps through finding rational ways to handle their past ordeals.

Chapter 3

Mariri in New Zealand

After returning from WW2, my father started a transport company back in New Zealand. My sister Catherine was the firstborn, followed by myself in 1948, then Diana. Catherine knew plants grew by watering them, so she thought that perhaps I could grow like a plant also if watered; she promptly gave me a good dose with a hose in my pram. I did not sprout wing shoots like a plant, but I am still trying to learn how to fly. Fortunately, it was a cane wicker pram, she says, otherwise it might have filled, but one cannot blame the little darling, as she was only small and trying to help.

Dad became tired of the transport company, so we moved up to the northern end of the South Island to Mariri, between Nelson and Motueka, where he bought a 25-acre apple orchard. Our home was on top of a hill looking over the sea, with Motueka fronting across the bay and snow-capped mountains behind us...such beautiful scenery. We have revisited the property, and it is still in excellent condition. It was so picturesque, with an acre or two of luscious strawberries 100 metres or so behind the house. We would walk down a steep track and cross a busy road to the tidal area. My father carried us across channels in the mudflats to an island nearly a kilometre from home. One day when the tide receded, we discovered two large fish stranded in a pool nearby, so we promptly took them home in a bucket.

One day, when crossing the road to the bay, I did not notice the school bus coming around a bend in the road, and it just missed me by a few inches. This was a fortunate escape. **Psalm 23:4 (NIV) says, "*Even though I walk through the valley of the shadow of death, I will fear no evil, for you are with me; your rod and your staff, they comfort me.*"** This is in David's conversation with God, where David shows faith that God will save him; He can save us too.

One of Dad's orchard friends, Charles, was also a soldier during the war and was captured by the Germans. He had three boys and a girl, the youngest named John, who was a close friend. **One day I borrowed John's gumboots to have a wander out on the mudflats, and when walking near one of the channels, the boots went down, and I was not able to pull my feet out due to the suction, however hard I tried. Anyway, the tide was coming in quickly, and I began to realise that if I could not get out, I could drown, being only seven, mind you. The water started to flow around my body, so panicking and yelling set in — thinking I was going to lose my life. Blood started squirting from my** nose. It gives me the horrors just remembering this experience. Anyway, being exhausted and still calling for help, the water was now swirling well up around my body. Guess who should come along the road but one of Dad's orchard workers, who ran out and pulled me free just in time. *Oh boy*, that was a close one—and traumatic. Surely God had sent this man to pull me out, as he arrived just before the sea was about to engulf me.

It was not God's time for me to go yet! See **Psalm 18:6 (NIV)**: *"In my distress I called to the Lord; I cried to my Lord for help. From his temple he heard my voice; my cry came before him, into his ears."* In addition, read **Isaiah 43:2 (NIV)**: *"When you pass through the waters, I will be with you; and when you pass through the rivers, they will not sweep over you. When you walk through the fire, you will not be burned; the flames will not set you ablaze."* Also read **Psalm 40:1-3 (NIV)**: *"I waited patiently for the Lord: he turned to me and heard my cry. He lifted me out of the slimy pit, out of the mud and mire; he set my feet on a rock and gave me a firm place to stand. He put a new song in my mouth, a hymn of praise to our God."* How true these verses were for me, especially the last one—thank you, Lord.

When harvesting time came, we used to help in the packing sheds located down on the shores; amid the delightful smell of apples and new pine packing boxes, various-sized apples being graded, mesmerizing as they rolled along a conveyor belt. We had a charming old cocker spaniel dog called Wad, and he followed us everywhere, even keeping between a dam and us where Mum and Dad told us there was an evil serpent, just for our safety, to keep us away.

One of Dad's cows passed away from eating too many unripe green apples. Another time Diana and I sneaked down to the strawberry patch and filled our little tummies with as many strawberries as we possibly could. Luckily, they were not green apples. In addition, Dad shot two rabbits with one shot, to my amazement. One wonders what the rabbits were up to...having a good old chat maybe: "*Hmm, rabbits will be rabbits*"! So they say, poor little fellas—what a way to go!

One day, Catherine and her friend dressed up as witches and chased Diana and me; Diana was so afraid that she left a deposit in her pants. Thinking it looked a bit like a bag of Dad's apples, it prompted me to say, "*Don't worry, I will look after you, Baggy*", and of course, that nickname stuck with her from then on! We still laugh about those times, and Diana is a good sister, with a great sense of humour, a strong determined spirit, and a kind heart. I used that name "Baggy", (said with fondness) occasionally, especially later in life, when she gave me a clip around the ears after our cat jumped off her lap, scratching her legs. The cat was frightened by an explosive bang from an attempt of mine to remove a small stump down in the backyard, which shook the house, causing a barometer to fall off the wall, which startled the cat. Of course, one does not blame her. The cat was probably a nervous wreck, especially after trying another harmless trick on it to discourage it from attempting to eat my pet budgies I was trying to breed for pocket money.

Because of Dad's excellent service during WW2, he was asked to serve in the Korean War, which loomed while we were at Mariri. They requested he lead a large New Zealand contingent to Korea; however, as he had had enough of war, he politely declined, to which they then asked him to serve in Parliament, but he declined again as he was a farmer at heart. He dressed up in his army outfit to go and talk with them about whether he would serve. Thinking that he was going off to serve in the Korean War, we shed tears as he waved goodbye, never forgetting that moment and how smart he looked.

Along came Guy Fawkes Night when they used to have a colossal fire at the Mariri sports grounds, and Mum and Dad had made a Guy Fawkes to throw in the fire. Well, sitting in the back of our old Ford next to this ugly creature as my company for the journey was so frightening. Having that creep next to me was like a scary dream, so guess who had to be left at home—and it was not me. I was not too popular that night.

Mum and Dad had many old 78 records, which included songs like "The Donkey Serenade", "The Desert Song", "He Played His Ukulele as the Ship Went Down", "How Much Is That Doggy in the Window", and many other popular old songs, some of which we still have, and they played them on an old "His Masters Voice" gramophone. One never forgets some of the old popular songs they used to play. We find good music is very therapeutic and is important for balance, lifting one's spirit, happiness, and joy in one's life. My mother always gathered us around the piano throughout our lives, where we enjoyed singing our hearts out. These were wonderful times.

We had an old T model Ford, and Dad drove it up to sixty miles per hour one day, not bad for an old car with sideboards and a crank handle to start it. One day a friend called Sandy from Motueka visited us and decided to do some tinkering with our old Ford. Well, Sandy was a rather mischievous little fellow. His name suited him; he fiddled and played with all the gadgets and buttons, and you guessed it! The battery went flat, so one vaguely remembers Dad cursing a little and having to jumpstart the car down the hill. Dad said we were not having Sandy to stay again.

We often went to church in Motueka and occasionally spent the day at Kaiteriteri beach, a beautiful spot with picturesque headlands, beaches, and small islands. Walking around the colourful rocks on the headlands was a favourite pastime of mine. One day on the way back, my sister Diana accidentally closed the car door on my fingers, severing my middle finger. It is fine now, though, after having it sewn back on by a doctor.

As there was a gold mine near Mariri, Dad took a job helping in this mine when work was quiet in the orchard. It was next to a rocky riverbed running down from the mountains. Going there and looking down a large, deep black mine shaft going vertically, seemingly forever, was a bit scary as I leaned over it and thought, "Gee, it would not be pleasant falling down there." It had water seeping in, and the pumps of the time were not strong enough to lower the water level; as they said, there was gold down there the size of one's fist, and they could not get at it. Recently, as pumps improved, their story proved correct, and they recovered gold from the mine again.

At one stage, we stayed at Picton just east of Nelson around the coast on the Marlborough Sounds, where the green lip mussels come from. In this area, they also produce quality wines, principally Sauvignon Blanc. In the Sounds, we went fishing, catching the tasty blue cod and occasionally octopus, which had a habit of putting their suckers on one's arm. Putting my first caught blue cod near my pillow now seems funny, but catching it as a child was so exciting; however, by the morning there was a bit of a pong. Can you imagine it? Being a fishing fanatic from then onwards came naturally, although the fish are put elsewhere nowadays. Diana had more luck catching the bigger ones.

Picton was, and still is, a delightful place, and trying to race the large steam trains home was exciting. They left from Picton and puffed their way along the hillsides to gain height to go over the range. The house we stayed in at the time was near the track, so racing back from school to see the trains toot and puff by was a thrill.

Steam trains had wonderful sounds as they puffed their way through the tunnels on the way, and standing next to their enormous wheels left one looking like a dwarf. Having a soft spot for the old steam trains was undeniable; there is something magical and alive about them, like big beasts, as many others testify.

Apple sales were seasonal, the market was sometimes unstable, and one year, Dad and many other orchardists had to pick the apples off their trees and leave them on the ground, as there was no satisfactory market. Finally, Dad and Mum decided to sell our orchard. We only received about 700 pounds for the property. It sold for more than a million pounds later. Heaven knows what it is worth now, and we still feel Dad did not receive the true worth. If you were to sell such a property today, buy a typical-sized home, and invest the rest, perhaps you might live comfortably on that.

Stuck in the mud with my gumboots at the age of seven during an incoming tide. Saved just in time when the water was up to my neck.

Chapter 4

Amberley in New Zealand

I remember travelling in our trusty old Ford with everything hanging off it, including the dog, like the car in the funny old American *Beverly Hillbillies* show, and we travelled three hundred miles south, back to Amberley near Christchurch, where our cousins and grandmother lived.

Memories as a child going to stay with our Aunts, who were some of Sam Coleman's children, at Riverside near Amberley, are unforgettable. They were wonderful old ladies whose names were Aunt Em, Aunt Alice, Aunt Mary, and Aunt Doll, and they loved having us children stay with them. At the Aunts' place, after receiving a small wind-up Hornsby train for Christmas and excitedly un-wrapping it, it was admired for hours. Later it was set up for target practise with an air rifle as it chugged its way around the track. Poor little thing, it had a few dints after this, like some of us.

However, it set me up to be a crack shot later in life, which most likely saved a friend's life.

Riding my bike three miles out of Amberley, where the old steam trains passed, was most enjoyable. I would ride out past our school into the countryside, past the old Cypress and stone and yellow flowering prickly gorse hedge fences. When going down to the river with Aunt Mary one day, upon arriving, she started digging near a weeping willow on the riverbank. She said to me, "Johnny, come and see what your Aunt Mary has found." I thought to myself, "Oh it could not be sunken treasure, that's only in pirate stories", yet it was sunken treasure of sorts; she lifted up a container and pulled out a huge wad of pound notes. Later I found out from my cousins that the Aunts hid money from each other. That is cash in hand for you.

There were old outer buildings and scenic gardens full of flowers and walking tracks. One led to a cold store with a door built into the side of a cliff that was under some shady trees. This is where they would keep food and goods before the invention of refrigeration. We could walk farther on to their beehives, then on down to a picturesque meandering stream called the Kowai River, its source originating in the mountains. Riverside was close to where my father lived on a farm, where Uncle Philip, Leah, and their children later lived. There were green meadows adorned with willows, poplars, elms, pines, and Australian gums. Samuel Coleman brought these gum trees from Australia to North Canterbury, and they grew well in the area.

Autumn brought a blaze of yellows, oranges, and reds in the trees to the landscape, and there was often snow covering nearby Mount Grey in the background. We loved picking the abundant mushrooms when they were in season, although we had to avoid the big red ones with white spots on them under the pine trees. Our Aunts would cook superb fresh scones on the old iron stoves. With homemade butter, they were very tasty.

One day we went swimming in a river just north of Amberley. Being about eight, and watching adults walking and swimming in a large pool, for some reason I thought it was shallower than it was. Dog paddling out to one section and trying to stand where it was out of my depth, I realized there was no bottom, which was a predicament. Going under, looking up, and losing some air from my lungs was not pleasant. Immediately my thought was to reach the surface to get air. Then I went under again, going down and ingesting more water, and panicking to the surface, only to go under again. Just when I was losing the plot, God said to me, *"Go to the surface, and start dog paddling to the shore."* With another desperate effort, I reached the surface and miraculously did as told. I spluttered my way to the shore, and God saved my life.

The adults were all completely oblivious to what had happened. I felt angry with those adults who had not helped me, but I eventually realised that they did not notice what had happened. Another nasty experience—saved again. **Isaiah 43:2 (NIV) says,** *"When you pass through the waters, I will be with you; and when you pass through the rivers, they will not sweep over you. When you walk through the fire, you will not be burned; the flames will* *not set you ablaze."* This was the second time this verse or promise applied to me, still only being about eight. In the past, there was reluctance to mention God when reflecting on what has happened, but not anymore.

Sometimes our families would get together at the beach at night, and the men would drag a net along the beach and bring it in bouncing with fish, namely herrings and New Zealand Kahawai, which in Australia, they call sea salmon, although it is not the true salmon. A sack dragged behind us along the beach filled with fish in no time. We also went white baiting, where we would set a small net in the shallows of a running river near the sea and come home with a pound or two of tasty whitebait, a small, thin, whitish fish, delicious in an egg omelette.

Going hunting in the snow-capped mountains with Dad and his friends was memorable, and we stayed beside a lake in an old cabin, where we sat around a fire having a yarn. The next day we saw salmon jumping up waterfalls in a river running down from the mountains. Shortly after, I was running after Dad as he chased a wild boar, shooting it on the run with his .303 rifle. It was risky for me, as an open pocketknife was in my hands.

There were also red deer in the mountains, which my father's brother Ken occasionally shot for food as he farmed in the hills. This venison was tasty, with a gamey flavour. Later the New Zealanders developed deer farms to capitalize on its popularity. Exportation of venison is mainly to Europe, and the antler velvet is an export to Asian countries for medicinal purposes.

We went to school in the snow sometimes, and there were ice covered puddles, old inkwells on the desks, milk for morning tea, and an abusive teacher, who loved to whip our legs, bruising them badly with his cane for the smallest mistake, even talking for a second to a classmate; can't win, can we? I developed a fear about this person; his abuse would certainly not be acceptable nowadays. Forgiveness is the best medicine for these hurts, despite being difficult to do at times.

One of the higher classes declared war on our class, so we had a catapult battle down at the Kowhai River, and it ended by seeing us tied to the trees for a few hours. We were afraid they would forget to release us and that we might rot there. Fortunately, we were using gum nuts some of the time in our catapults, but the things we did in those days we would not dream of doing now.

Another favourite pastime was climbing through the large Cypress hedges along the roads. Some friends, Rennie and Geoff, would remember these activities. Sometimes we would go with the family to the horse races and bet on a horse. Some of our cousins, especially Philip and Leah's family, Carol and Philippa, are still keen on horseracing and have their own horses trained. The day that we went, I put a penny or two on a horse after it came first. Guess where it came in the next race. You guessed it—last. That was my first lesson in gambling, perhaps a good one.

Our neighbour's son played with bows and arrows and one day shot an arrow straight up in the air out of sight. After a number of seconds, suddenly, *bang*—guess where it hit? Yes, right in the middle of my noggin. Fortunately, he had put the nail in backwards, and the blunt end pounded my head. It nearly knocked me out, with blood everywhere, but thank goodness it was not the pointy way up. I am slightly amused about that now but was not at the time it happened. Fortunately, it did not hit my eye or finish me for that matter...*ah, saved again.*

At other times air-rifle pellets were whizzing close to my head as I climbed our walnut tree and when going down the road on my bike. Using me as target practise seemed to be one of his favourite pastimes...such a dear little boy. See **Psalm 23:4 (NIV)** and **Psalm 34:17–20 (NIV)**.

Rugby at school was enjoyable, and once we were playing demonstration rugby at the Domain, where they also held shows. I also enjoyed being in the Cubs for quite some time. This is a form of scouts for younger boys.

Nearby we visited our friends, who produced tasty honey, especially creamed honey and honey in the honeycomb. We still keep in touch with Diana's nice school friend Neroli from that family.

Occasionally our family would go to Christchurch and wander through the picturesque Avon gardens or climb the stairs of the spire of the old Christchurch Cathedral, now sadly collapsed because of the horrendous earthquakes in Christchurch recently, with the loss of many lives and severe damage to old treasured buildings that gave Christchurch its personality. Aunty June, Dad's sister, being quite shocked about the earthquakes, mentioned that my maternal great-grandfather, the master builder, built many of Christchurch's older buildings. June sadly passed away recently in her nineties. She was a remarkable person, and we all admired her very much.

We also travelled to Lyttelton Harbour, a scenic landlocked harbour that was the mouth of an old volcano. The masts of old sailing ships still protruded from the water. This is where we departed for trips to the North Island on the ships *Hine-moa* and *Maori*, of around eight thousand tons each; sailing through the night, arriving at Wellington the next morning. Fortunately, we were not on a later ship called the *Wahine*, which was badly damaged in a storm just out of Wellington with the loss of many lives.

Having enjoyed those trips, my love for the sea has subsequently developed. Memories are of staying at a hotel with a naturally heated pool, where we swam at night, looking over Lake Taupo. Here we witnessed one of the volcanoes *Mt. Tongariro*, erupting, with its reflections showing strikingly in the lake. Nearby were large geothermal bores roaring away like enormous steam trains; nowadays they are harnessed for electricity. We passed through large pine forests followed by fishing with friends for trout in the Tongariro River, where Dad and his friends caught five- to seven-pound trout. Being small at the time, when holding the fish, they reached from the top of my head to my feet. I felt like saying to them, "How dare you be bigger than me?"

Then we went on to Whakatane, where we were entertained with an unforgettable Maori concert. The women threw their Pois around divinely, and the men threw their arms around while doing the Haka war dance. Whakatane was notably where the Maoris first settled after arriving in Aotearoa (which means "Land of the Long White Cloud") as the Maoris then called New Zealand, seeing the long stretches of snow-capped mountains; when they arrived from the Hawaiian Islands in their outrigger canoes more than six hundred years ago.

Chapter 5

Holidays in New South Wales, Australia

At the age of eight, we went for a holiday to Australia in 1956 and stayed on a wheat and sheep farm near Forbes with Mum's brother David and his mother as well as with Mum's sister Olive and husband Frank and their family. We also visited her brother John and wife Amy and their children, Jan and Jeffrey, at their farm. This farm was the original family farm where Mum grew up. The land was flat, ochre-red in colour, sparsely covered with the odd gum and native pines, casuarinas, wheat paddocks, and the occasional tree-covered hilly areas. This was near the tramping grounds of the Bushranger Ben Hall, whose sad experiences brought about what unfolded in his life.

This area was such a contrast with New Zealand and could be cruel or unrelenting in drought times, yet it had a special beauty and quality, which I still love. It had its own special spiritual qualities. Its quietness was only interrupted by the sound of galahs, or crows, in the distance, and the stillness of the evenings was very special as we gazed into the clear skies at the Milky Way, spotting the odd shooting star. The magic of the countryside of Australia remained in my heart, and later this was expressed in my paintings.

I could understand why Mum loved this area. It was away from the cities, so clean, pure, quiet, and safe. I could feel a spiritual presence in this area, and quiet country places like these away from the city can help one relax and reconnect with God. When we stayed at Aunty Olive's we saw the Aurora Borealis in the night sky and were fortunate enough to see the first Russian Sputnik satellite pass over.

The first air rifle I owned was a Diana 16, and my sister with the same name shot yours truly in the backside with it one day, just for fun, but my poor backside thought otherwise; it was just like a big nasty ant bite though. Air rifles were legal to own at a young age then. Quickly becoming a good shot, it held me in good stead for future hunting trips.

When wandering off over the hills with the air rifle, a pack of tiny foxes suddenly appeared near a hollow log, and they were like cute little puppies, so I didn't take a shot but just admired them playing. I hope they were not a problem on the farm later on.

This was an enjoyable experience, somehow a spiritual one, which encouraged further hunting expeditions. It was just getting away in the hills, which were so peaceful, not the shooting part but just feeling free.

The outback farmers have developed the personality and strength of character as well as a sense of humour needed to cope with the harsh times and droughts, which prevail sometimes for years. One could see this in my uncles and aunts, David and Margaret, John and Amy, Frank and Olive, and their families. Something special about these people prevailed. They had a personality many of us Aussies have grown to love in our country folk.

While staying at Frank and Olive's home when eight, I came down with tonsillitis, which produced a dangerous temperature of 104 degrees; it was not a pleasant experience. My mouth was full of ulcers, and fortunately, Mum and Olive organized her kind girls, Wendy, Helen, and Sylvia, then teenagers, to sponge cold water on me and feed me. I will never forget their kindness and attention, and I believe they helped save my life, so I am deeply grateful. God helps us especially through people. **(Psalm 23:4 NIV and Psalm 34:17–20 NIV)**

One of the girls caring for me, Sylvia, is the mother of "Brax" in the series *Home and Away* on television, his real name being Steve. He is our cousin of whom we are proud. He acted with the best of them in a movie called *Hercules*, filmed in Budapest. My sister Catherine had a special trip from New Zealand to Australia as a ten-year-old and went to school with Sylvia, his mother, as they are a similar age. The family also helped me when I worked in NSW as an assistant superintendent of Parks and Gardens.

One can attribute God's love coming through this family. Olive had a difficult life, as she later lost two of her lovely girls, Wendy through cancer and Helen in a car accident, and later her husband, Frank. We will never forget Helen, as she was a wonderful entertainer. She did the Charleston dance so well, and she sang superbly, especially one of the songs Pat Boone sang, "Love Letters in the Sand".

Losing part of their family surely affected them, yet their Christian values and attitudes to life, especially Olive, have helped them carry on. Olive lived into her 90s with many grandchildren and great-grandchildren of which she was so proud. We enjoyed attending her 90th birthday at Forbes, where many friends and family attended. She was still bright and alert at that age, but as she passed away a few years ago, Sylvia, Colin, and Doug, her children will surely miss her.

We all had many fond memories of our younger days with this family, playing tennis and many other activities on the farm as we visited them from Melbourne after moving from New Zealand.

Chapter 6

Our Move to Melbourne in Australia

Dad, working as an agricultural advisory officer around the Canterbury district, came to Australia and travelled up the east coast into Queensland, exploring the work potential in these areas, and finally decided to move to Melbourne, where he accepted an agricultural position with the company Dalgety. Our family boarded the steam train in Amberley and said our goodbyes to our cousins and aunts, who we would surely miss. As the steam train puffed its way to Christchurch, sheep would run in the distance whenever the train blew its whistle. If we put our heads out of the window, we were anointed with the black, smelly soot from the smoke funnel—all part of the joys of a steam train ride.

We then boarded the 10,000-ton ship *Wanganella* at Lyttelton harbour, bound for Sydney. The ship was charming inside with magnificent old carved wooden decorations, pillars, and furniture. Going to breakfast one morning, it was so rough we were tossed from side to side in the walkways as if we had one too many. I felt seasick as the waves were enormous, rolling over the front of the ship. Portholes went well under the sea as the ship rolled, and food flew off the tables. I doubt very much if the poor old ship had stabilizers at that time.

Going onto the deck one day, I remember it taking all my energy just to open the door. I was almost blown away entering the deck walkways exposed to the sea and winds, so I held on tightly to the rail as I watched mountainous seas rolling past, probably thirty to forty feet high or more, and their troughs were like deep valleys. It was an extraordinary sight. The force of the wind was so strong; it was quite dangerous, but somehow thrilling. Then somebody told me off and said, "You had better get back inside; you could be blown away!" Forcing the door open against the wind to go inside again was difficult. It would have been even difficult for adults out there.

The seas calmed, and we spent some pleasant times on deck sipping beef soup, nowadays called Bonox, and watching the albatrosses, large birds that can fly long distances across the oceans. The journey of four days passed quickly, and when coming into Sydney Harbour, the Harbour Bridge dwarfed the *Wanganella*. This was a memory one never forgets. The Opera House was non-existent at that time. We then met and stayed with Uncle Horace, who had worked valiantly for the farmers as a Federal MP when younger. (*See The Nationals, Senators and MPS from 1920*)

Our Move to Melbourne in Australia

We then travelled to Melbourne and rented a place at Bonbeach. We started school and soon became Aussies, learning their ways. Television had just started, so we were in on the act with only a small black-and-white television, which we were mesmerized by sometimes.

We eventually bought a home at Montmorency on a slope looking over bush-land. Dad put in a chicken pen and vegetable garden. We went to Montmorency State School, and I did some watercolour painting, inspired by my mother's watercolours of New Zealand scenes and by Albert Namatjira's paintings.

Joining the school marching team was a good discipline, and we had rigorous training by our devoted headmaster, who would froth at the mouth training us; however, it was not in vain, as our school won the Victorian championships for five years in a row.

Some friends, Ray and Owen, and I enjoyed going to the Plenty River to explore and fish for Redfin with worms and usually a float. Our other activities were collecting birds' eggs. We became expert climbers and scaled the largest trees to get those elusive eggs. We would climb high; one slip and it would be all over. It was dangerous sometimes, but we did not even entertain those thoughts of height; we just did it despite the dangers, slippery limbs, and so forth. Mind you, falling eight or ten feet once and spraining a foot badly was quite painful actually, so perhaps it was a lesson. We would name the eggs of the bird species and keep them in special wooden boxes for display, proudly comparing each other's efforts. This was a popular pastime in those days.

Our bikes sometimes left much to be desired with poor brakes, which made going downhill dangerous on the way home from school, especially at the bottom of a particular hill. It required making a ninety-degree turn as the road took this angle. We were thankful for a small emergency road that kept going up the next hill.

One weekend, Owen and I, aged eleven at the time, decided to ride our bikes from Montmorency to the Healesville Sanctuary. We pedalled our way across creeks and over mountains at Yarra Glen, one of the areas that had burned in the most recent severe bushfires. When going through Yarra Glen and heading for Healesville across open plains, two teenagers of about 15 with a .22 rifle stood in the middle of the road pointing the rifle at us, a genuine holdup. They told us to hand over our money, and as we refused this request, they bashed us, robbed us, and sent us on our way down the hill. We pedalled our bikes for all our worth, but it was in vain, as they started shooting the .22 rifle at us. Twenty-two rifles are dangerous business, and if hit with such a bullet, one could die instantly. There were bullets whizzing past my body and through the frame of the bike, so close, yet saved again by the Lord. Read Ephesians 6:16 (NIV): *In addition to all this, take up the shield of faith, with which you can extinguish all the flaming arrows of the evil one.* In addition, read **Psalm 23:4 (NIV)** and **Psalm 34:17–20 (NIV).** See also **2 Thessalonians 3:3 (NIV):** *"But the Lord is faithful, and he will strengthen you and protect you from the evil one."*

We went on our way and were so determined to see the animals at Healesville Sanctuary that we thought we would put off telling the police for a while as it was about mid-afternoon, and we did not want to miss out. I guess we were devoted greenies to such an extent that we did not report this incident immediately. During the evening, we rode back towards Ringwood to find an easier way home, but it was getting dark, so we thought we had better visit the police, where we told our story. They rang Owen's parents, who picked us up. What a day!

Not long after, we were wandering around an old sand quarry, and Owen became caught in quicksand. He started yelling and going down, so I quickly grabbed an old branch, and having to walk out onto the sand myself, I began to go down but managed to pull him out, much to his relief. *Phew! What a close one.* Read **Psalm 23:4** and **Psalm 34:17–20**. It was a lesson for us not to wander around quarries; mind you, we cannot remember seeing any *Keep Out* signs.

We often had meals with Graeme and Marion and their children Mark, Matthew, and Julian, in Eltham. Marion was a very talented oil painter, and Julian is now a famous watercolour artist. Graeme's mother was named Florence and was the sister of Dad's mother Catherine. I would often play chess with Mark, but as he was a champion, I did not hold out against him for very long. Sadly, Graeme passed away recently; he was a great person who always knew the benefits of a good laugh.

Chapter 7

Teenage Years

When around the age of fourteen, archery became a favourite hobby. The stories of Robin Hood and Davy Crockett always fascinated me, and I enjoyed reading about true history battles with bows and arrows and crossbows, such as "The Battle of Agincourt" and "The Battle of Poitiers", where the old English longbow helped win over vastly superior numbers of armoured knights on horseback. Making a crossbow from plans in an old encyclopaedia was a challenge, but I cut out the trigger mechanisms, wooden stock, and the bow lengthwise from a leaf spring from a car with hacksaw blades, which took some perseverance. Many blades became blunt with this project; however, the crossbow worked admirably, and I held it with pride for many years. I joined clubs and became a reasonable shot with the bow and arrow, winning prizes at a later age in archery club competitions and bringing down wild pigs with another crossbow as well as with a hunting bow.

I took out a large wild pig, dropping it where it stood with the crossbow, when hunting with friends having rifles, who were skeptical about the crossbow's potential, but then amazed by its power. I brought down another boar with a hunting bow on another trip with a friend, Steve. However, at an earlier time, when using bent wooden arrows, I just nicked the side of a very large, aggressive boar, which I gathered annoyed him somewhat, promptly warning me to look for the nearest tree when he started to charge. From then on, the only option was the very straight aluminium arrows, no longer wooden ones. I also spent some time in a Scout group, which inspired my learning about camping, bush tucker, and living off the land. This toughened us up and threw in some discipline, all good fun.

We bought a piebald horse of fifteen hands in height named Kim. He stayed nearby, and we fed him with chaff and oats regularly. He was a rogue, though, as he would get out of the old fenced paddock and explore the district for a few weeks. I once found him as far away as Hurstbridge enjoying some apples in an orchard, where the unamused owner found him, which was embarrassing. It was amazing that we ever tracked him down; I must have had a good nose. Once when saddling him up, he bloated himself, not desiring to go for a ride, put his head between my legs, and threw me through the air for about three to four metres against a shed—one powerful horse. Another time he rolled on top of me and once trod heavily on my feet.

Then one day, when riding Kim towards a train crossing a railway bridge, he became startled and reared up. My body flew through the air, sliding along the top of a passing car and finally landing on the road without any serious bodily damage. What a miracle! One could have easily landed in front of the car, which may have been a different story as the car was travelling at about 30 kilometres per hour. It is most likely a fact that most horse owners have stories like these to tell. Saved again, see **Psalm 23:4 (NIV)** and **Psalm 34:17–20 (NIV)**.

Another time when cantering up a hill on Kim, he decided to pass under a tree with a horizontal branch just at stomach height. The branch connected amidships, taking me swiftly off the back of the horse and winding me badly; I eventually staggered to my feet after a few minutes of gasping for air on the ground. It sounds funny now when reminiscing but could have been more serious. I was wondering what else this dear horse had up his saddle.

This happened on another horse that had a mind of his own also. He bolted—I was not able to hold him back—and he went straight for a barbed wire fence and abruptly stopped, but not me, as you can imagine. I went flying into the next paddock across that barbed-wire fence. He was one powerful, nasty horse…I will not say what I thought of him when brushing the skid marks off my backside. It is remarkable what our bodies can take at a young age.

Occasionally I raced Kim against other horses, and this is the only time he would get off his butt and start galloping; he actually enjoyed the challenge. When jumping him across a raised wooden bar, I ended up in some prickly blackberry bushes nearby with several decent scratches as painful evidence. From then onwards horse jumping was definitely out of the question as a future hobby.

One day when riding Kim, I had a predicament in crossing the Plenty River, where there was a human, or horse, footbridge next to the car bridge. Well, there was continual traffic on the road; so accordingly, the car bridge was too risky for Kim. Being in a hurry, I decided to lead him across the footbridge, which appeared sturdily built, mind you; however, when we were halfway across, where it was about thirty feet or more down to the river, Kim started to panic, and the footbridge started to sway badly from side to side. This was dangerous, so reassuring him was necessary saying, "Calm down, you old...or we will both end up in the drink." He slowly calmed, thank goodness, so we made it to the other side. This could have been another disaster, although the bridge undoubtedly looked sturdy enough to take a horse. See **Psalm 23:4 (NIV)** and **Psalm 34:17–20 (NIV)**. Yet having a horse was so enjoyable, and selling him was quite sad. I later found out that he was renamed Satan. They got that one right, although he was not bad really; he was just a rogue with a sense of humour, like some of us. I am sure I had not influenced him inadvertently; his character surely must have developed predating my ownership, hmm?

While at high school, I was involved in a Gilbert and Sullivan production called *The Gondoliers*. Catherine my sister was also in Gilbert and Sullivan Productions, one being *The Pirates of Penzance*. These were excellent productions and nearly equivalent to professional ones. Also during my high school days, I developed a crush on a girl called Rhonda after she invited me to dance at one of our high school dances; I was fond of her for years. However, after she left high school from fourth year, she married, which was a disappointment for me.

Chemistry became an interest at an early age, so the end of our shed became a laboratory of sorts! For some reason, we became interested in making volatile mixes and other potions, as many other boys did in the past. These were not to cause harm but more for the fascination, and one of the concoctions we mixed was placed in a long tube. It was fired off as a rocket, travelling out of sight at great speed; however, one day one of them blew up as it passed through a gum tree and blew a large amount of leaves off it, making it look like a sad autumn tree preparing for winter. Dad happened to be watching, and as he had seen bombs go off, he said, "Gosh, just like El Alamein."

We also made homemade muskets, which worked well. We would not dream of doing such things now as one could severely damage oneself, so I do not recommend doing these things. One day when grinding powders in a pestle and mortar in the laboratory, not knowing about its flammable nature, it caught fire rapidly, singeing all the hairs on my arms and head as well as the person next to me, making us look like ducks singed over a fire ready for the pot. Luckily, it did not explode. *Phew, that was a close one.* Read **Psalm 23:4 (NIV)** and **Psalm 34:17–20 (NIV)**.

When we were young teenagers, having seen monkeys sent into space, we thought we could carry out a similar operation, so we built a rocket with a cosy compartment to make sure it was safe for our little astronaut mouse and placed him packed in plenty of cotton wool before sending the rocket skywards. After reaching a little altitude, it returned to earth, and after opening the hatch, our little friend marched out quite happily with his little head held high. I thought I heard him say, "See, I told you I could do it... now where is the best cheese in the land and a wee drop, thank you." Consequently, he was our little hero. God is good that He also loves our little friends.

Friends from high school and I went on a number of camping trips on our bikes; once out to the Healesville Upper Yarra dam and another time to Warburton. One of our bikes was a tandem for two. I ran out of leg power on my bike and was not able to turn the wheels anymore when approaching Warburton, which miraculously happened outside a milk bar. A tasty meat pie was a most welcome treat, and it reenergized me enough to reach our camping spot next to the Yarra River just out of town. This was a delightful area, with the Yarra River winding its way through the autumn-coloured trees dotting the lower hills.

When ferreting and hunting for rabbits with friends, the ferret nearly bit my finger off (charming little creature). I cannot say what I called him. I felt like testing his neck for elasticity. We would go for miles out around farmlands and along the Yarra River, looking for rabbit burrows. We put the nets over their holes then introduced the ferret into their burrows. Once the rabbits heard the approaching ferret, they would run for their lives, only to run into the nets.

Teenage Years

We would often come home with about eight rabbits, and if the ferret happened to find a rabbit, it would stay down there, and we would be outside in the dark, twiddling our thumbs, waiting for our dear little mate to show himself again. We would try to call him with "where are you" in as nice a way as we could muster, which was difficult. When he emerged, he was fatter, with a big grin from ear to ear and that look of satiety, while we were starving. He was quite lucky we did not eat him actually. In those days, rabbits were food, and some communities around the world still have to do hunting like this for their survival.

We went to stay near Grenfell on a farm, which I was told belonged to people related to Rod Laver, the famous Australian tennis champion. The woman owner was one of Mum's best friends, who had nursed soldiers with Mum in Sydney during the war. They had a tennis court there, so we had a few games. There was an old large King James Bible, highly decorated with intricate illustrations done in the 1800s; it was fascinating. They took us out on horseback around the hills to check their sheep, and this was an exhilarating experience, especially as the scenery was so inspiring. In the distance were green hills covered with groups of gum trees and boulders all arranged in nature's perfect order. There were occasional willows growing along a picturesque blue stream, meandering quietly between the lower reaches of the hills. It was such a delightful spot, and taking painting gear to the side of the stream to capture its beauty on canvas was an inspiration. These were wonderful experiences.

Taking a .22 rifle into the hills for a shot, was an experience, as there were so many rabbit pests, and taking out my most incredible shot ever undertaken was unforgettable. I had to raise the sights, fire, and after walking for what seemed like a quarter of an hour for hundreds of metres across a valley, I came to my prize. The sights of the rifle covered a gum tree the rabbit was sitting under so far away. A scope on the rifle would not have done a better job.

Although I grew up in the Church of England, where Mum and Dad would take us, I cannot remember much. Getting up and down in the cold wooden pews to pray in winter was rather annoying, to say the least. Yet with the occasional pretty girl in the next aisle to cast a kindly smile on, well, that was just about it—oh, except for that little nip of port up at the front to remember the blood Jesus shed for our sins—so these were some of the things I remember.

That was almost the limit of my Christian knowledge at that stage, yet it was sowing the seed of faith, as I remember a picture of Jesus on the wall of the church touching me spiritually; there was something special about it—perhaps the look of compassion and understanding on His face. In addition, being in a youth group gave us some enjoyable times. Later we tried Presbyterian and Methodist churches, and finally, the United Church. Although I prayed when young, it was only after going through severe losses when the Holy Spirit touched me that I looked to God more earnestly.

During the school holidays, we spent time sometimes at Dee Why, near Sydney, at my grandmother's home looking over the sea. We would go there to see our cousins, Mum's elder sister Peg, and her large family. We used to take the surfboard and spend many hours down at the surf, unfortunately getting badly sunburnt mind you. We also enjoyed going fishing around the rocks. One day there was a rip in the surf, and hearing a girl calling frantically for help farther out on a lilo yours truly swam out and pulled her back in, swimming against the current, which was quite exhausting. We enjoyed those days in the sun, though, and developed a lifelong love for the sea as well as respect for it.

Another time we went with friends to stay at a farm cottage at Bright, another picturesque place where the Ovens River winds its way through valleys and hills, close to the snowfields. We spent our time hunting rabbits, trout fishing, and going to the snowfields for fun while learning to ski. One particular day at the snowfields was memorable, as I got my skis tangled up with a girl's skis when learning the art. She was from the family we went with. I do not know how we did it, but our skis were so tangled and facing in all directions that we ended up lying on the snow together laughing our heads off as we tried to untangle ourselves...oh the joys of skiing.

Wherever travelling as a teenager, I would take photographs of pleasant scenery, take sketches, or even paint on the spot, as I was fond of the bush, mountains, rivers, and scenery.

Having bought a tiny 1930s Austin 7, we drove it around Dad's farm block for many years as teenagers. We cut logs to build a log cabin and towed them with the poor little thing until its axle broke. One night with friends, we decided to go hunting along the back tracks in the bush. The front window of the car opened out like a home window so that we could aim the shotgun straight ahead. After telling my friend to be careful not to shoot the car by mistake, what should happen, when a fox ran in front of us, he fired. In the excitement, he missed the fox but not the car. A few pellets skimmed the top of the radiator, much to my dismay—not much damage though luckily. It seems funny now when reminiscing! These little cars are worth a fortune nowadays, and it only sold for about 10 pounds then, which is equivalent to about 20 dollars, but that was close to the price we paid for it.

After doing some painting training under a well-known Eltham artist, who emphasized getting tonal values correct from the beginning, I did a correspondence course with Stott's, successfully completing a certificate in "Oil and Watercolour Painting". Later, I completed a "Diploma of Commercial Art", after about two to three years of consignment work. From then on, I had greater success in selling paintings and using them as gifts.

After having an art exhibition with a few other artists when 19, painting became a forte, and I found much joy and fulfilment in this. Becoming involved in painting boosted self-esteem and gave me a lifelong interest and hobby. When becoming involved in painting, I would completely lose myself; my spirit would take over, and this was the most joyful and fulfilling time. It was one way of tuning in to God. When this happened, the creation of my best paintings occurred. Having developed a love for nature and the beauty of the New Zealand and Australian scenery gave me immense fulfilment while expressing it in paintings. I desire to express and show this beauty God has created for our benefit, knowing we need this for serenity in our busy lives. I am grateful to God for this gift.

The peaceful and relaxing side of nature, such as water scenes, are predominant in my collection and are created for people to meditate upon, and thus help relax and rebalance themselves, especially during stressful times. Therefore, I desired to somehow help my fellow man find relaxation, peace, and joy in life, praying that my paintings would help do this. My sister Diana also does excellent watercolours.

When around eighteen, taking a job during school holidays working on a farm in Northern Victoria gave me valuable farm experience milking cows, feeding pigs, driving tractors, spraying paddocks, and so forth. Although one day when spraying pig manure on the paddocks with a tractor, the wind blew it back in my face, much to my disgust; it felt and must have looked rather dirty—well, nothing that a good long shower and a mouthwash gargle wouldn't fix.

Working in a chocolate factory with a friend for part-time money on the school holidays again was an experience to remember. The sight of enormous containers of chocolate, and chocolates of all descriptions everywhere, was so mouth-watering. One felt like diving into it all due to the divine smell. Who cares if we came out looking like chocolate Smurfs?

Another time at the same age, I hitched rides in cars (as many did in those days) from Melbourne to Noosa Heads in Queensland with two friends, Robin and Peter. Sometimes we had to split and agreed to meet at certain places at specific times. We stayed overnight in Sydney and spent the New Year at Coolangatta.

One night in Coolangatta provided us with fascinating lightning with fireballs in the night sky; it was a remarkable sight, which we have never seen anywhere before. When we arrived at Noosa, it was only a small country town with a hotel on the hill, and we slept overnight in the sand hills on the main beach, which nowadays have resorts and shops built on them. The night was perfect, so it was very pleasant watching the moonshine glittering across the sea and sleeping with the sound of gentle waves rolling in.

On the way north, a chap picked me up with a hotted-up Holden, which had a triple SU carburettor. We stopped for a snack, and after buying a milkshake, he took off at great speed, and half the milkshake was spread across my face and clothing. Oh great, as if it had not been shaken enough I felt like telling him. Well, talk about a hair-raising experience; soon we were travelling at 136 miles per hour (about 219 kilometres per hour) for a long time. It was like the vision you get out of a racing car, and when going up a mountain, he nearly wrote off a motorbike rider and us; I was thinking time was up to hop out before it was too late. This was dangerous driving, thus being another risky time for me. When he took off, he burned so much rubber from his tyres that one could not see his car; it had extraordinary power but silly brains behind it, which can be a deadly combination. **Psalm 23:4 (NIV) and Psalm 34:17–20 (NIV).**

Then on the way home, a Volkswagen picked me up, and the driver drove off the side of the road through the trees, just missing some. I said to him, "What are you trying to prove, hmm?", and his friend said, "Oh don't worry, he's only on LSD." Would you believe it? I guess you can imagine what I asked him to do shortly afterwards: "Let me out thank-you." That was another dangerous time. When would it ever end? When nearing Canberra, a truck driver picked me up and said he was so tired but needed to get back to Melbourne, so he asked me to drive his truck, almost the size of a semitrailer, mind you. We had many other interesting experiences, but I thought I might mention these.

Remembering the joys of going to the Diamond Creek or Yarra River, where I rescued a little possum (shown on the back cover), and throwing a line out for redfin, roach, or other fish species, where we used worms or dough, sometimes with a float, we mesmerized the float going under, which often seemed to work. Then we would take the fish home, and cooking it was the ultimate. During these years, getting into the mountains with an old Lithgow single shot .22 rifle hunting, climbing, camping, fishing, and exploring, especially after long examinations at college, was rejuvenating to the soul. Somehow, God would revitalize me through spending time in the mountains after the hectic life of the city and study. Visiting a rifle range where they were target shooting with special target .22s was interesting. A few rounds with some regulars and a close to 100 win was almost to my disbelief; perhaps I should have kept it up.

One day, a close encounter with a tiger snake occurred. It reared its angry flattened head, somewhat like a Cobra, its tail hidden by the grass, most likely under my feet. It struck with a known striking speed of around 72 miles per hour towards what was previously a weight on its tail. Fortunately, I anticipated its purpose when its head rose, and jumping quickly

sideways, its strike missed me by a few centimetres. I was a fortunate boy again, having read that one drop of a tiger snake's venom could kill 220 sheep—one of the deadliest snakes in the world. I would not fancy that in my system. *"Phew", saved again.* This incident happened when we were living in Victoria (Psalm 23:4 NIV and Psalm 34:17–20 NIV).

My friend Algius and I decided to go hunting for pigs in New South Wales. We drove in next to the Lachlan River after savouring a few pig shooting tales at the nearby watering hole with the locals. This was followed by getting my trusty little Morris-Minor bogged, then a tow out with a local's 4-wheel drive. We finally set up camp and took off hunting. Fortunately, we took coats and a box of matches, as we had walked so far down the river that we decided to light a fire and sleep next to it for the night rather than go back to our tent.

The next morning we arose with the sun and headed off optimistically, rifles in hand. We had not gone far when we came across a large boar I thought was as big as a small rhinoceros (well almost, ha-ha); anyway, I silently raised the .303 rifle and fired. He fell where he stood, but his leg gouged a large hole in the half sun-baked clay ground. We cut the tusks off him, which were quite long, and one of his hind legs for food. He was so heavy we could hardly lift his backside off the ground, and we were strong eighteen year olds.

After a short walk, I managed to wound another large boar on the run at around 60 metres. After chasing this pig for some distance, it was obviously very annoyed at us and decided to turn on

Algius, who was firing at it with an old WW2 Italian rifle. It was only a few metres from him, charging towards him with nasty long tusks, so I only had time for a shot from my hip with the .303, and the pig ploughed towards him and fell dead at his feet. It could have finished him without this quick shot. Wild pigs are very dangerous and have mortally wounded many hunting dogs. **Psalm 23:4 (NIV)** and **Psalm 34:17–20 (NIV)**.

There was a time of bad bushfires around the surrounding areas of Melbourne, the Dandenong ranges, and the Yarra Valley. I was at high school when they had broken out. A friend had many horses and asked me to help him rescue them. There also were many men volunteering to fight the fires along the Yarra Valley, so we volunteered, and I joined hundreds of men in a fighting line with wet sacks, branches, knapsacks, and whatever we could, get our hands on.

At one stage, the wind died back, and we could go among the gums and bushy areas to beat out residual flames, but the wind suddenly came up strongly again, and flames were roaring through the treetops towards us. It looked nasty and dangerous and was unbearably hot. We were coughing and choking in the hot smoke, and many were saying run for your lives, which we did; many men jumped into a dam, but the rest of us had to run through tall, dry grass with flames hot on our tail. Fortunately, we reached the road, with flames soaring behind us, nearly singeing our backsides—another close one. Read Isaiah 43:2 (NIV): *"When you pass through the waters, I will be with you; and when you pass through the rivers, they will* *not sweep over you. When you walk through the fire, you will not be burned; the flames will not set you ablaze."* This is a promise of protection from God.

My father was away in Gippsland working, and a fellow with exactly the same name as me had lost his life in the flames in another fire not far away, so Dad came back frantically thinking it was me. Many people lost their lives, and many homes were lost in these fires.

During my high school years, pursuing many activities apart from study was fulfilling, and I enjoyed athletic activities and playing tennis at school, winning a few small trophies in a club and playing in the high school championships at Kooyong. I also participated in running and long jump high school competitions, in which I would sometimes come in second or third and once first in my form for gymnastics.

In an experiment, I accidentally mixed the wrong chemicals; a reaction occurred and gave off brown acid fumes, and as I had a bad cold, I could not smell the toxic fumes. Well, I inhaled those fumes. Can you imagine the pain? I bent over coughing and could not breathe. This was a horrible experience. An ambulance arrived, and I was put on oxygen, but from then on, I couldn't remember going to hospital, only waking there feeling as though my lungs had been burned out. This was another close miss for me and one that damaged my health, as I never felt very well for a long time after this experience; it affected the quality of my life for years ahead. However, learning to become tough and developing fortitude

and persistence in life carried me through, but it was not easy. Psalm 23:4 (NIV) and Psalm 34:17–20 (NIV).

Another time I went for a spin as a passenger with a friend, Ross, and others in his open Jeep. After going off the road and running into a log hidden by long grass, nearly breaking our knees on the dashboard, he then decided to put it out of gear and roll down a dirt road. It lost control and slewed sideways, throwing us all out on the side of the road. *The next moment or second, I looked up to see the Jeep coming down on top of me; the right front wheel came straight down towards my head, but it was prevented from crushing my body by a branch of a tree.* God saved me again surely. Psalm 23:4 (NIV) and Psalm 34:19–20 (NIV). *"A righteous man may have many troubles, but the Lord delivers him from them all; he protects all his bones, not one will be broken."* Not that I was so righteous, yet the Lord had a purpose for me. An old man walked along the road and said, "These darn trees are the problem"; I suppose you can imagine my answer to that. I have been a tree lover ever since.

After finishing fifth year at high school, I went on to Burnley Horticultural College to study for a "Diploma in Horticulture", which took three years plus three months of work experience at a native plant nursery to complete. My sister Diana also started at the college simultaneously as I. Our love of nature, flora, and fauna led us on this voyage of discovery.

We had around fourteen subjects. Can you imagine doing two and a half hour long examinations for that many detailed subjects? My head felt hot from activity after these, so a good break was well earned. We spent about forty per cent of our time out gaining practical experience in the nursery, vegetable crops area, parks and gardens, and orchard with its many species of fruit trees, where we used tractors, spraying, and mowing equipment for orchard maintenance. It was a good all-round training course.

I developed a fondness for a girl at college called Ann, a pleasant, quiet, and rather shy girl, and we went together for a while. We went on church camps to Wilson's Promontory with our Church of England youth group, with whom we had wonderful times singing around the campfires with guitars, hiking, and having get-togethers. Members became lifelong friends, especially Michael, Arthur, and Diane.

One night we went ice-skating with them to St. Kilda, and I was moving around well after gaining some confidence on the skates. Somebody's leg got in my way, and I went down, hitting my forehead on the ice. When I came to after the knock out, I was in the first-aid room, where they were applying ice to a bruise the size of a small ice cream on my forehead. Sometimes concussions like this can cause damage, which has occurred to footballers and boxers.

We had several excursions away in the college truck, where we packed in like sardines. One of our expeditions was to the Tatura Research Station, where we learned about new orchard practices. These included more efficient pruning techniques, and many other new innovative tree care practices. Some of us had to speak about a particular subject we had specialized in, in groups. We had special accommodation and eating areas. This was during the time of the Vietnam War, when "flower power" was all the rage and hippies were saying, "Make love not war". I was around 19 when they had compulsory conscription for military service, where some had to go to Vietnam having no say in the matter; however, some, called conscientious objectors, avoided it by arguing for their rights.

They drew our date of birth out of a barrel, so to speak, to decide who had to go. I remember Dad saying, "I hope you do not have to go to that nasty jungle fighting war." Although my date was in that barrel, like many others, they missed it, fortunately perhaps, because many Vietnam veterans were damaged psychologically from the war and from the treatment, they received when they came back.

At college, a friend Russell, and I, took off for the Flinders Ranges in a small Austin A30 I had at the time. I think the tank only took about six or seven dollars' worth of petrol, and the cruising speed was only about 45 miles per hour, or close to 72 kilometres per hour. It tested our patience over long distances; however, it did an admirable job, only getting its sump scratched while crossing a rocky creek bed that was part of the dirt road.

The Flinders ranges were beautiful; a purplish blue with plains covered in wildflowers, broken only by the occasional rocky outcrop and ghost gum endowed creek beds, which are popular in many paintings done by the famous painter Sir Hans Heysen. He was my favourite artist, whom I wished to emulate, thus my camera and paintbox were my treasured possessions. Wilpena Pound and Brachina Gorge were two of many memorable spots in these ranges, which have inspiring scenery.

We had college hiking and camping trips, one to Wilson's Promontory, providing magnificent scenery along the hiking tracks, especially at Sealers Cove. We also played in football matches and tennis at the college. At the time, I bought a hotted-up Morris Minor car, metallic blue, with wide tyres, a wooden dash with a built in tachometer, a hotted-up MG-A engine with ported and polished valves and a three-quarter cam, and a large chrome exhaust pipe exuding from one side. It sounded more like a large motorbike revving up than a car engine. It had won a drag for its class at the drag championships, so you can imagine its power.

Unfortunately, they had only upgraded the brakes to those of a Morris Major, still far from sufficient. It was probably a blessing in disguise that the big end bearings in the motor became worn and noisy on a trip back home from Eildon Weir. The car managed to crawl home with a sad engine at 30 miles per hour, once being capable of quite a lot more. We found another MG-A motor to put in the car, as fixing the big end bearings would be more expensive. It only had half the power and the brakes were a worry, so it was goodbye to this little monster.

When fishing one day out on a point that ran a kilometre or so out to sea from the northern end of Safety Beach, an incoming tide washed some valuable gear out past the rocks. Thinking, well, I cannot see any strong current, so I should be able to get back easily, I headed out after the gear. After grabbing it and turning around to swim back, I found I was up against a very powerful current. Oh no, another drama unfolding, and swimming against this exceedingly strong tide

became exhausting. Not being able to make headway against it back to shore, I decided to swim in another direction, and luckily, I gradually approached the rocks away from the point. Making it back was exhausting fighting the current with all the strength I could muster. Without changing direction and God especially, I surely would not have made it back. Isaiah 43:2 (NIV) says, *"When you pass through the waters, I will be with you; and when you pass through the rivers, they will not sweep over you. When you walk through the fire, you will not be burned; the flames will not set you ablaze."*

These times found me trekking the foothills of Mount Buller, fishing and shooting. I was climbing a gully one morning and walking through some tree ferns near a mountain creek when something charged out, taking me by surprise and nearly knocking me over. You would not believe it, but it was an enormous Sambar deer with huge antlers, running so close. I had not experienced buck fever until then, but I quickly opened the bolt of the .303 and shoved a bullet into the breach. The deer had run uphill for about fifty to sixty metres and stopped behind a gum tree. I needed his other end, but all I had was his rear end visible, so I had to aim at the most vulnerable part I could think of.

The shot passed just slightly over his shoulder, and I did not get a second chance. I aimed at him with a slight touch of buck fever as they call it, making me squeeze the trigger slightly faster than normal; this being the reason for missing. Getting a Sambar deer in Australia is an achievement, and I regretted missing it, but that is life and perhaps was meant to be; *I do not mourn this loss any more, having changed my values.*

At Mount Buller, our campsite was right next to a fast-flowing stream, and it was so pleasant sitting around the campfire at night chatting and curling up in a sleeping bag, lulled to sleep by the sounds of the stream with its little waterfalls nearby. Many years later, I could have lost my life in this area in the oncoming dark on the foothills of snow-covered Mount Buller during winter in minus 10-degree temperatures, having to spend the whole night in the bush in temperatures as cold as a freezer. I will elaborate on this later.

Soon after leaving college, I met a lovely girl called Judy at a dance in Heidelberg. We spent wonderful times together, and she was such a sweet, special girl to me that I fell for her and about a year later proposed to her, to which she agreed.

I took a position as leading gardener in the Eltham Shire Council, where we were involved in routine care of parks and gardens in areas around the shire, including landscaping work and constructing large boulder retaining walls.

Snorkelling and spearfishing with friends near Melbourne was a favourite pastime, especially at Point Leo, where we usually had a good catch. One day when invited, I could not go for some reason; anyway, to cut a long story short, a large shark rounded up my friend Jeff on that day. He only just made it to a rock protruding from the water. It would have been too bad for me if I had been behind him. He told me the shark went around and around that rock, as in the movie *Jaws*. I was lucky to have had other plans;

I would not fancy being the main course for the day, or even hors d'oeuvres for that matter; thank-you, Lord, for giving me a reason not to go that day. See **2 Timothy 4:17 (NIV):** *"But the Lord stood at my side and gave me strength, so that through me the message might be fully proclaimed and all the Gentiles might hear it. And I was delivered from the lion's mouth."* See also **Proverbs 3:5–7 (NIV),** where it says, *"Trust in the LORD with all your heart and lean not on your own understanding; in all your ways acknowledge him, and he will make your paths straight. Do not be wise in your own eyes; fear the LORD and shun evil."*

My rogue horse takes me off by a branch in the stomach.

Teenage Years

My bolting horse from a train scare throwing me onto a fast passing car.

Saved by a branch when I was under a friends overturned Jeep.

Chapter 8

Change Around the World

During my late teenage years there was a remarkable new movement and change in society, one of questioning and challenging our ways of living and old ideas. It involved the teaching of new philosophies and the cultivation of alternative ways of living. One could see this desire for change and self-expression in art and music (such as the music of the Beatles). During the sixties and seventies especially, people were analysing their existence and realising the way things were did not bring fulfilment. Even people with highly paid positions— doctors, engineers, people in all occupations—were giving up their secure jobs and lifestyles to try to find their Utopia.

They often bought up land and returned to simple living or joined new communes, similar to the one formed at Nimbin, where they were trying to find peace and fulfilment. Some found this to a degree, but others came in and relied on others' efforts. A certain amount of work was still required, but whoever had a particular skill used it to help others and traded their skills for the other person's skill instead of using money. This was a type of barter trade. It was an interesting time, and some still live this way of life.

People brought in many new ideas and philosophies, meditation, and Eastern ideas, especially religious ones. We were fortunate to be in a country such as Australia where we had the freedom to express ourselves and explore new ideas. For example, one of the more natural and efficient ways of producing more food on small acreage evolved using a method known as Permaculture. This is a technique used by some Asian countries for thousands of years, where a property is designed to recycle by-products, such as water and manures from livestock, birds, fish, and animals. The by-products help grow crops, such as vegetables, grains, herbs, and fruit trees, which are all planted carefully according to a more natural layout that is more efficient and productive on small acreage than older, conventional methods. It is a great idea, especially for small farms and communes and even the home garden.

Because of my interest and study of science and nature, I became concerned about global warming, climate change, and its danger to the human race. The Holy Spirit compelled me to discuss this, including other problems our civilisation faces, so that we can all help in their resolution.

Many scientists believe human-created global warming is causing many problems worldwide. Most scientists now have sufficient evidence to show that global warming is creating extreme weather and temperature changes, droughts, massive bushfires, crop failures, and sea level rises. These rises are starting to inundate areas along the coasts of many islands, as testified by the islanders themselves. Combined with fighting and wars, it is adding to the problems of mass migrations of people due to insecurity, diseases, hunger, malnutrition, and starvation, causing many deaths. We should all pray and try to help these people, to the best of our capacity. Positive prayer with faith is very powerful, especially when practised by many people.

These problems, including pollution and global warming, are concerns that some disbelieve, but scientists have gathered much evidence to support the reality of this danger. Although I am not an expert on this matter, I have read a number of books written by scientists. One I especially recommend is *The Revenge of Gaia* by James Lovelock, a renowned highly acclaimed and qualified scientist (see Grey, John, 2006), which is compelling reading. Basically, Lovelock says Gaia is the earth's physiological life balancing system to keep life healthy. (I believe this is obviously created by God.) He says we have messed up this balance, and the earth, in this respect, is ill. He says the earth is like a body, and if we become the disease, it will try to eventually control us unless we separate ourselves from the earth's balancing mechanisms. To do this while maintaining large populations, according to information in his book, we would need to change our ways, and energy sources he says, and cut back on traditional agricultural and fishing practices, producing some of our food artificially. This would be a pity for our palate and tastes, but with help, he says, it might give the land and seas a chance to regenerate. Being a well-qualified scientist in this realm of expertise, his book is written with much detail, knowledge, research, and concern for the future.

After reading both sides of the argument, I concluded, like many others, that global warming is real. It has been said, to be very dangerous for future human populations. It has come about through the need to support huge populations, a desire by all to have a better lifestyle, but also greed. However, the scientists say the excess carbon and methane build-up will most likely cause dire consequences for our quality of life, unless we do something about it. Methane, which has a much higher global warming potential than carbon dioxide, is being released in large quantities in the Siberian Arctic Tundra areas due to warming and melting of the permafrost, which has previously had the methane trapped. Huge plumes of it are being discovered in these areas rising from the permafrost and have many scientists worried about the consequences. (See Wikimedia Foundation Inc., 2014)

Also the IPCC's latest report says that methane is thirty-four times more powerful than carbon dioxide over 100 years in its heat trapping or global warming potential; however, it said it is eighty-six times more powerful over a twenty-year period (See Romm, Joe, 2013). So switching from coal to gas from the new gas fields is not the answer either, he says, as much methane is lost even from the most carefully built gas fields.

Newer carbon-free power production methods and new alternative energy systems, such as solar, wind, wave, geothermal, and so forth—along with education of the world's population—are necessary to help stem the tide of these problems. The creation of all our materialistic possessions, such as large cars, large houses, and all our gadgets, requires the burning of large amounts of fossil fuels to produce the power required for their production. This enormous demand is giving off too much carbon dioxide, creating global warming.

To put it simply, the excess carbon dioxide and methane create a glasshouse effect, trapping the sun's radiation and heat, warming the oceans, acidifying them, and influencing the currents and their temperature as they flow around land masses, thus affecting climate and rainfall patterns. This is the reason for more extremes in weather. It only takes a slight amount of carbon dioxide and temperature change, so the earth's life balancing mechanism is quite delicate. The earth has always undergone changes, but changes normally taking many thousands of years have occurred within a little over one century due to man's activities. One can see the receding glaciers around the world, especially in New Zealand and Greenland, since the time of the Industrial Revolution. I feel compelled to mention this problem because ignoring it could be disastrous for future populations. We can all make a difference.

In addition, the use of pesticides, chemicals, and antibiotics is creating superbugs and further possible dire consequences, such as upsets and imbalances to human health and to our important insect populations, especially bees. Bacteria are becoming more resistant to antibiotics, one reason being many people do not finish their course of medicine, giving the few stronger, surviving bacteria a chance to regenerate. Also many of our food species, including many farm animals, are given antibiotics, creating the same outcome; we have to resolve these problems. Genetically modified food (GMO food) is one of great debate as well, and *release implications* should be checked concerning safety for humans and our insect population. Future viable seed access, including that of old original strains, should remain. There should be studies relating to all possible outcomes, including economic forecasts before release. Some seed releases have been a success and others a danger.

This is a complex issue, but it is an important one I feel needs mentioning. These are just a few examples of many very important issues for humankind to tackle logically, scientifically, but always firstly with prayer for guidance in making the right decisions. The Bible is a book of eternal wisdom and guidance and cannot mention every problem encountered in the future, yet God would expect us to apply it's teachings to our present day circumstances and dangers, such as those mentioned, for our benefit and the earth's. I believe one should not remain restricted in one's way of thinking but remain open, not departing from the word, with a spirit of discernment. I believe we cannot just say leave it up to God when we are creating something we have to take the consequences for. Actually, it is good to see that many Christians are changing and becoming educated about taking care of the earth and all of God's creations. There are many sites on the Internet and books written to testify to this truth (See *"A scriptural call for environmental stewardship"*). God has given us the power to resolve or destroy; it's up to us. He will be there to help clean up the mess we create and say to us, "I warned you." Sometimes important decisions can only be made after research with the facts, which requires wider reading of qualified, proven material, especially with prayer.

In the Bible, the Lord has asked us to take care and be stewards of our planet and all living creatures on it; it is the only one we have, and our future generations would expect us to care for it. It is not really fair to leave it in bad condition for our children and theirs. See warnings in **Revelation 11:18 (NIV)**, where the Lord says in part, *"for destroying those who destroy the earth"* and **Ezekiel 34:18 (NIV):** *"Is it too little for you to have eaten up the good pasture-and to have drunk of the clear waters, that you must foul the residue with your feet?"* See also **Leviticus 25:23-24 (NIV):** *"The land must not be sold permanently, because the land is mine and you reside in my land as foreigners and strangers. Throughout the land that you hold as a possession, you must provide for the redemption of the land."* See also **Jeremiah 2:7 (NIV):** *"I brought you into a fertile land to eat its fruit and rich produce. But you came and defiled my land and made my inheritance detestable."* And see **James 5:5 (NIV):** *"You have lived on earth in luxury and self-indulgence. You have fattened yourselves in the day of slaughter."*

There are many verses in the Bible for us mentioning care of the earth and its creations, so I believe it is time well spent in learning about ways in which we can help save our planet; even just turning off the lights, using less power, and choosing smaller cars, if possible, is a great help. It is such a shame to see beautiful places such as the Amazon Basin on our planet dwindling away and other areas under threat through heartless destruction of beautiful forests, landscapes, and our beautiful Barrier reef due to global warming, greed, and desire for capital gain. There needs to be a balance, a change in the use of resources, even if that costs us in one way or another.

The other concerns for us are wars; usually between those with ulterior motives such as greed; following dangerous belief systems, and accusing other religions of being false and evil, or using verses out of context, creating an excuse to fight; yet in comparison, our Christian Faith is good, as are some other religions, only praying for all to strive for peace, love, acceptance, patience, understanding, and harmony between one another. People in different cultures have certain belief systems with differing perceptions of God and how they think God expects them to behave. However, some belief systems can be false in God's eyes, thus causing disharmony between creeds, for God said in **Isaiah 2:4 (NIV)** *"Nation will not take up sword against nation"*; this being the word of God, should be heeded, and help enable the banning of very violent computer fighting games and movies; for they affect the vulnerable minds of many young people in a negative way, only adding to the violence already surfacing with disastrous results around the world. God is a God of love, not war, read **John 5:29 (NIV)** where it says, *"and those who have done evil will rise to be condemned"*, and in **John 14:6 (NIV)** Jesus says, *"no one comes to the Father except through me"*, also Jesus said in **Matthew 26:52 (NIV)**, *"Put your sword back in its place," Jesus said to him, "for all who draw the sword will die by the sword.* And in **Romans 12:19 (NIV)** it says, *Do not take revenge, my friends,* *but leave room for God's wrath, for it is written: "It is mine to avenge; I will repay," says the Lord.* Surely this is the way towards harmony between races. People that believe problems will be resolved by fighting have been deceived by the evil one, as fighting and lack of forgiveness only brings sorrow to those who carry bitterness in their hearts.

Masses of people can be brainwashed by those with ulterior motives of greed and power. A number of people in most religions have brought some degree of discredit to their religion, turning one against the other and these actions are usually from individuals within a religion breaking the laws. God is not to blame nor should He be rejected for their crimes against others. We should also forgive one another amongst different religions for what has happened in the past, for we are not really to blame for what our predecessors may or may not have done. We have grown in wisdom, and learnt from the mistakes of certain individuals many centuries ago, so we should be careful not to be influenced by those who may say to the contrary, for our Christian faith through the New Testament in the Bible promotes peace and love amongst all people, which is God's desire; this surely being the only way to achieve peace, for Jesus said to love our enemies, see **Matthew 5:38:45 (NIV).**

All people should sit down and talk to resolve problems, forgive one another with an understanding of man's weaknesses, learn and grow towards knowing the importance of an attitude of peace, and replace greed with an attitude of generosity. Those with false attitudes will never achieve peace by fighting. I really feel we should all pray more for peace in the world as we find solutions to these problems and try to live in harmony, acceptance, and understanding of one another's differences while trying to teach about Jesus to those who need to learn the truth for true salvation.

We are all spiritually connected, and therefore we should be living in harmony with one another by knowing that it is the evil forces, whispering bad intent in people's ears, not other humans, see **Ephesians 6:12 (NIV)**. The evil realm is fooling vulnerable and even intellectual people by using clever, manipulative people, who themselves have been misled, often having bitter hearts and distasteful attitudes towards another race or creed. They train with propaganda and false information, some used out of context, their actions and policies only creating wars between creeds, however God prefers give and take with love, tact, negotiation, diplomacy and grace, not force with the sword, which has never brought peace.

The attitudes they create can spread quickly amongst many people, creating what the people think is an accepted truth. We should all be aware of these deceptive techniques and guard and protect ourselves from the evil one doing this amongst our fellow men, especially vulnerable younger people. This fact should influence us all to live in peace with one another. We all grow up in different societies accepting what we learn as the truth; yet some information can be false, and some is true; depending on what we are taught, read, and hear from others within our society, there is always a chance that some of it can consist of bad propaganda. We must all develop discerning spirits. I recommend knowing Jesus and reading the word as it teaches us how to live in harmony, in peace, and with joy, keeping the evil one at bay.

In **1 John 4:4 (NIV)**, it says, *You, dear children, are from God and have overcome them, because the one who is in you is greater than the one who is in the world.* This means that the real Holy Spirit in you through acceptance of Christ Jesus is greater than the one who is in the world, which is the evil one. I have been compelled to mention these matters by the Holy Spirit, as it is just so important for us to learn more about the issues in this chapter so that we can help to resolve them; this is important for our future quality of life and humanity's future survival.

We should all try our best with respect to these serious issues facing humanity, for taking positive action in one way or another, with genuine concern is being an effective mature Christian, which should be our aim. We can all make a difference, even as individuals. I believe we should all aim towards our higher good by improving our relationship with God our Father and learning the Truth from Him with reference to the word from the Bible.

Chapter 9

A Trip to New Zealand

During my early twenties we went to New Zealand for a holiday and stayed with June and David and their family and spent time with Dad's brother Ken on his farm in the mountains. **With a borrowed .303 rifle and while looking for deer on Ken's farm, I approached the edge of a large cliff. I looked down on a scenic river with a gully running at right angles up the other side. I decided to have a look in this valley; however, when coming back up the home ridge, it started snowing, and my riding boots slipped many times in the snow and tussock grass while trying to climb the ridge.**

It was very chilly, and by the time I reached the top, I could hardly feel my legs or feet and could barely walk. The numbness was a strange feeling from the upper legs down, so deciding to quickly light a fire to thaw out under some shrubbery was a wise move, yet getting back to the homestead in a

hurry, before they sent out a search party, was of utmost importance. My arrival was just in time. Despite the snowstorm and the extreme cold catching me, I apologized for being overdue. I was fortunate to have had matches, as trying to walk with feet you cannot feel is very difficult. God's help was there again. See **Psalm 23:4 (NIV) and Psalm 34:17–20 (NIV).** This was the first time a box of matches possibly saved my life. Fortunately, I had read to carry matches when hunting. It actually happened the day before my twenty-first birthday. After arriving back in Amberley, we celebrated my birthday at Philip and Leah's home.

Sightseeing was a necessity, so I borrowed my grandmother's old car, a small model C10 1937 Ford, plus Phillip's .303 and headed off around the South Island of New Zealand. I travelled through Ashburton, where Mum's cousins lived on a farm, and where we had stayed as children. Mount Cook was my destination, where I stayed the night. The little car crossed a riverbed and then went along a road on the side of the Tasman Glacier, set at the foot of Mount Cook, the highest mountain in New Zealand. The front cover of this book shows a picture of Mount Cook, which I feel is very spiritual in a certain light, when the darkness at its base merges with the light at its peak, and portrays as a wonderful reminder of our aspirations and desires to reach for the heavens in our lives, as in the song, "Climb every mountain," in the movie "Sound of music." It has a height of nearly 13,000 feet and is very dangerous to climb, many having lost their lives on its slopes. Sir Edmund Hillary, a New Zealander, did his training on this

A Trip to New Zealand

mountain in preparation for his climb of Mount Everest, which he was the first to conquer.

After parking the car on the side of the road, right next to the glacier and at the base of the very steep sides of Mount Cook, I looked up at the snow-covered rocky slopes into the heavens to the top of Mount Cook. It seemed to go on forever like a giant pyramid reaching up and piercing the clouds. It undoubtedly looked formidable and made one appreciate how tiny we are on the scale of things. Sleeping the night there was without problems—except a Kea parrot, which kept me company in the morning and shared my cereal without my permission whenever I looked away. However, I now realise I stayed in a dangerous spot after hearing of rock-falls, avalanches, and 30 million tons of ice breaking off the Tasman Glacier during the Christchurch earthquakes. These crashed down into the lake, creating waves 3.5 metres high. So now I realise I could have been between the "devil and the deep blue sea" as the expression goes. However, one is never to know when these things may happen.

The next day I travelled on to Queenstown. On arrival, the car slid several metres down an ice-covered road. I travelled on around the lake road to the end of Lake Wakatipu and camped the night at the backwaters of the lake in a scenic valley full of beech trees lining a mountain stream. After waking in the morning, a small creek, and waterfall had frozen over that I slept next to; luckily, I was not. In fact, I cannot remember the cold bothering me there. I noticed the cold more when arriving back in Melbourne. The morning saw me climbing the hills through a beech forest, up a small valley. Just when climbing over rocks, a red deer jumped out and ran past me so quickly I didn't get a chance to have a shot at him. After leaving the lowlands, I headed across the higher tussock plains and managed to see three deer running in the distance, too far for a shot with no rifle scope.

After checking out the sky rail gondola and a beautiful snow-covered mountain range, called the Remarkables, with Lake Wakatipu and Queenstown at their lower reaches, I travelled on around the Haast Pass to the Franz Joseph Glacier. Before reaching the glacier, I passed a helicopter on the side of the road with many deer, which had been shot, strapped over it. Nowadays they are farming the deer.

When climbing along the side of the glacier, large chunks of ice broke off inside its interior, sounding like cannon blasts. These can be frightening to hear for the first time. I spent the night in a small primitive hut with a woodstove for cooking and to heat water. The next day saw me heading up the coast through Greymouth and back across the mountains through Arthur's Pass. Mum and Dad had travelled in this same little car with June and my grandmother on this road shortly after the end of the war.

While browsing old photographs a while ago, I was amazed when seeing this little car in its heyday; it was smarter then. It went over Arthur's Pass, though, without a missing a beat. Mind you, the average cruising speed was only about 35 to 40 miles per hour (about 60 to 70 kilometres per hour) along a flat road. After our holiday in New Zealand, I was looking forward to coming back to Australia and seeing Judy again.

Chapter 10

Four Years in New South Wales

After some time with the Eltham Shire Council, a position presented itself for an assistant superintendent in the Parks and Gardens in Dubbo, New South Wales. I took the position, where I was in charge of several men, caring for the parks. I soon found that I missed my fiancée Judy and I only had a Holden utility, which I found too slow for travelling overnight from Dubbo to Melbourne to see her and our families. I would arrive exhausted on Saturday morning only to have to drive back on a Sunday night—driving all night—and then going straight back to work. This was not a very pleasant feeling because of the extreme tiredness, so I bought a Datsun 1600 sedan, which cruised at a much better pace; however, distance was still a problem along with tiredness.

One hot day, when it was around 110° F in the shade, we went to the surrounds of an open sports field with crowbars to dig holes for tree planting. We had to pound our way through rocks, and the crowbars were so hot that our hands burned. We had to go out without gloves, so I was not too amused with the chap in charge of this.

Another cold night, when I was renting a bungalow, it was so cold I put on a radiator away from the bed; however, during the night, a blanket fell too close, causing a fire. Fortunately, I put the fire out just in time as it was between the door and me. See Isaiah 43:2 (NIV).

At one time, there was a mouse plague in the area, and mice running over our heads would wake us at night. They would run across the roads in their thousands when driving on the highways and wreaked havoc around the grain silos…little pests.

Eventually I checked the newspapers for positions and applied for a research position with the CSIRO at Griffith, in New South Wales. This was closer to Melbourne but still a respectable drive. Our work involved irrigation research on crops such as maize and cotton and indoor controlled environment temperature studies on crop growth as well as laboratory analysis of leaf and soil samples from experimental areas on farms. We analysed the data statistically for any significant differences with a large PDP9 computer, thus enabling conclusions to be drawn for experiments. I often used the computer for leaf area analysis and other data processing work. I even used an old mechanical calculator at times, just before small electrical calculators arrived on the scene. Information was processed onto paper tape at that time with the computer. When larger quantities of information needed processing, we sent it to a larger computer in Canberra.

Studies of electronics, statistics, and the FORTRAN computer language were required while there, so I went to Canberra to do a short FORTRAN course. I often showed visitors around the research station, explaining the work scientists were involved in, including the importance of weather equipment. The research station held more than eighty staff, including many scientists, so it was an interesting time of my life.

Being keen on commercial art while living at Griffith, I completed a "Certificate in Oil and Watercolour Painting", and a "Diploma of Commercial Art" by correspondence, which took a few years to finish, but these courses helped with my technical knowledge in creating better paintings, which I found fulfilling as a hobby as well as for extra income. It gave me the experience I needed to do commissioned paintings for people from that time onwards.

One day I was gathering scientific data from a cotton farm and a crop duster plane came over, spraying not only the crop but me also. I tried waving, but he did not see me; he turned around and gave me another dose. I was trying to get out of there as quickly as possible but could not cross the rows. The plane turned around and sprayed me for a third time. I had sore eyes and headaches for quite a while after that experience. Either he thought I was a scarecrow or he was dreaming.

I also had to use other chemicals frequently, now banned, such as 24D, DDT, 245T, Dieldrin, Tryquat, and Paraquat, and a specialist doctor later informed me that these contributed to chronic fatigue syndrome (CFS) which showed up at a later date. Communities of people living near cotton crops have also suffered illness from crop dusting chemicals.

I was staying in a rugged boarding lodge, so I rented another cottage on one of the orange orchards. I varnished and cleaned up this cottage, as I was to bring my wife Judy to live there. I then went back to Melbourne for my wedding, which went well, and Judy and I had our honeymoon along the NSW coast.

After a few weeks off, we returned to Griffith. Judy took a position in the bank there as a teller, and we settled down and explored the region, sometimes going to the local church. The local Italian farm owners looked after us, bringing their farm produce, including tasty homemade sausages, bread, and fruit, to us. One of the wineries commissioned me to do a large painting mural placed at the end of a hall for one of their winery dances.

Another journey took us to Cairns, where we were unaccustomed to the high humidity; it was like being in a sauna. We travelled back into the ranges behind Cairns, and while travelling around a mountain road, I saw what I thought was a large log across the road, but it was moving—thus it dawned on me that it was a gigantic snake. It must have been more than seven inches thick, and its head and tail were well on either side of the road—what a whopper; we thought we would just stay in the car and wait till it went past, like a train, which seemed an eternity. I often wondered what its length was. I did not fancy hopping out of the car to give it a kindly pat on the head. Just imagine that!

I went on a hunting trip with friends to look for wild pigs. When travelling out of the town by car, in which I was a passenger, we had a nasty accident at night. We came over a hill, where the lights of a car coming the other way temporarily blinded us, and there, standing in the middle of the road, was a woman in the path of my friend's car. I jumped out and tried to revive her using my first aid training from the CSIRO, but she had died instantly in this accident. It was a terrible nightmare for me, a shocking sight, which I will not go into detail about, too horrible to talk about in a book; it took me more than a year to recover from the trauma and shock of this accident. I can understand how soldiers feel; the experience of this was far worse than any movie can depict. At the court-hearing, her family thanked me for trying to revive her, but she had an approximate 0.39 blood alcohol reading, so we suspect she might have been trying to commit suicide or didn't know where she was due to the high blood alcohol content.

While working on our experimental plots, well out in the irrigation countryside, I had a few close encounters with brown snakes. They came out in spring with the warmer weather and were prolific. They are fast moving and deadly, so one cannot outrun them. We would tip them out of irrigation pipes as we joined the pipes. I was sitting minding my own business on an outback dunny, as Aussies call it, and a snake came through the door. I am not sure who got the biggest fright, as somehow I think I finished up crouching on the seat in a fraction of a second, and I suppose the ungodly sight of me gave it such a fright, he turned around and shot through as quickly as he could. I don't know who got the biggest fright; I hope he was not too shocked.

Some of my colleagues in the CSIRO would joke about this experience with me, as you can imagine. Another day I was quietly having lunch in the shed with another chap, and I heard a rustling right under my chair. When I looked down, there was a very large brown snake curled up, about seven feet long. He could have bitten me at any time, but he noticed that we saw him and decided to slide away. There was chicken wire blocking his retreat, and his head got caught in the one-centimeter wire.

Another time, when heading south from Griffith at night, my car nearly drove into a freight train at a crossing as it blended into the surroundings and sky well. I could not see any lights along the width of the train as a warning nor was there any noticeable railway crossing or warning lights. When travelling at a regular speed, the train loomed quickly; however, the brakes were engaged just in time, and the car pulled up within metres of it. *"Phew, that was another close one."* Read 23:4 (NIV) and Psalm 34:17–20 (NIV).

Then one night when coming back from Melbourne while driving out of Finley near where the train incident occurred, I was driving around a bend in the road, and a semitrailer passing my car showered the front windscreen with mud so that I could not see anything. I was travelling at the correct speed for a winding highway, but there was a steep cliff on this bend, so I had to keep driving, trying to slow and drive around the bend on my memory, with no vision at all. I was lucky I did not drive off the edge, which was a miracle—saved again. God must have guided my steering through that bend. See Psalm 23:4 (NIV) and Psalm 34:17–20 (NIV).

On another trip back, a large kangaroo jumped right in front of the car, writing it off—the poor old kangaroo. This could also have been a disaster, as kangaroos have in the past jumped through the windows of cars and thrashed around inside. When travelling from Griffith to Hay and travelling at a normal speed on an open straight highway, a large mob of kangaroos crossed in front, and fortunately, a small gap in the mob presented itself to pass through—fortunate again. See Psalm 23:4 (NIV) and Psalm 34:17–20 (NIV).

Chapter 11

Our Trip to Darwin

Judy and I decided to go for a holiday around part of Australia and set off with tyres and gear packed on the roof. We headed for Melbourne then Adelaide. We went up along the Gulf, sometimes on dirt roads from the top of the Gulf onwards, camping as we went, finally arriving at Coober Pedy, an opal-mining town. Upon arrival, it was blowing a dust storm, and refilling the petrol tank was a hurried effort because of swirling dust trying to enter. We managed to stop for a while and see some opals and the local homes, all underground, cooler and neatly carved out of the rock. The high temperatures above ground contrasted with the steady temperature in these homes, which provide much relief from the heat and lack of shade above.

Finding some opals, mainly white ones, occurred on a later trip to Lightning Ridge in Northern New South Wales. We travelled on towards Central Australia across ochre red plains, passing rock and native shrub covered ranges, scrubby trees, ghost gums, and rocky outcrops with kangaroos and wild horses giving life to the landscapes. Bull-dust off the road was so fine that even with the windows up it would seep into every crevice of the car, our faces, and our equipment. It was very irritating in many ways, to say the least; however, we still enjoyed stopping, having a cup of tea (or cuppa as we call it here), and lighting a campfire near the side of the road at night. Nights were cold in Central Australia, but the days were warm during our time of travel. The view of the Milky Way with its vast array of stars was always magnificent as the skies were so clear.

We went out to Ayers Rock, named Uluru by the Aborigines of Australia. We camped there for a night and climbed it the next day, which was an amazing experience—like walking on an asteroid just above the Earth, a huge bare rock. An Aboriginal guide gave a speech about its history, showing rock paintings, and where waves and wind had shaped its contours in ancient times. We spent the next night camping at the foot of the Olgas called Kata Tjuta by the Aborigines, near Ayer's Rock, and we could feel the Aboriginal spirits around us while we were sitting around the campfire. Many people have said they had a similar experience. It is difficult to explain the experience; you just know they are with you.

The colour changes of the Olgas and Ayer's Rock were astounding to watch as they changed from subtle reds to deep purple-blues as the sun went down. This was an unforgettable experience visiting these areas. After visiting Alice Springs, we detoured out to some popular gorges where Albert Namatjira painted. As I mentioned earlier, some of his delightful paintings inspired me. The beauty and colour of the surrounding hills undoubtedly provided inspiration to him and were typical of his paintings. We went on to Stanley Chasm and Simpson's Gap, both such beautiful spots with their amazing red and purple cliffs and water features. We saw other popular spots and listened to dingoes howling on top of the ranges at night...eerie. We passed Aboriginal couples on horseback, and I asked whether I could take a photograph of them, to which they requested money; however, it turned out to be an interesting painting, and my photographs resulted in several paintings from this area.

We continued on to Tennant Creek, where surprisingly large circular rocks called the Devil's Marbles were sitting out in nowhere as though a giant had placed them there. While there, we visited one of Terry's brothers, Robin, and his family. Robin was teaching there at Tennant Creek. Sadly, Robin died later of cancer.

It took a week or more to reach Darwin from Adelaide, travelling long distances daily, and it made one realise how large Australia is. I definitely sympathize with Burke and Wills, the famous explorers, and their astonishing trip from Melbourne to the Gulf of Carpentaria and back to Coopers Creek by camel; how they must have suffered. It is just so far even by car and very hot at times. Due to their camels escaping and breeding in the wild, there are many thousands of them now roaming freely in Central Australia and the Northern Territory, where they are becoming pests.

When coming down through the hills to Darwin, we could pick up Indonesian or Malaysian radio stations on the car radio. After our arrival, we camped for the night at Fanny Bay and woke sweating in our sleeping bags at five in the morning. Darwin was a pleasant, picturesque, multicultural town, still not a large city when Cyclone Tracy flattened it a few years later so that most of Darwin needed rebuilding. On the way back, we cruised along Katherine Gorge by boat, spotting crocodiles on the shore, and were dwarfed by spectacular towering red cliffs on both sides, and picture-perfect reflections on the river. I thought what a paradise for Aborigines in the past, and there are many other wonderful landscapes like these in Northern Australia, with cascading waterfalls as cooling oases providing relief from often harsh and barren landscapes in some areas, especially in Central Australia and the Northern Territory. Yet despite this, these landscapes have a special beauty, unique only to Australia.

We went on to Mount Isa from there and had a blowout on a front tyre at normal speed; however, it was very difficult controlling the car and bringing it to a stop safely. A blowout on a front wheel at speed is exceedingly dangerous. We could have easily rolled over—saved again. See Psalm 23:4 (NIV) and Psalm 34:17–20 (NIV).

Chapter 12

Back to Melbourne to Live

After three years or so working in Griffith, we were getting tired with our jobs in the area, so we decided to move back to Melbourne. I had asked my parents to look for a home with some land I could work on, which they soon found for us to purchase. After moving back, Judy took a position in the bank again, and I took a position for a year or so just doing the night shift in a bread factory, putting trays of dough in a proofer, which helps the dough rise for baking in the ovens. After helping clean the equipment and factory, I would come home in the morning to sleep.

One evening some trays tipped out beneath their swinging carry-shelves, causing the proofer to jam. I immediately turned the proofer off and went to grab the trays out; however, somebody down the other end turned the proofer back on, unbeknown to me, as it moved quietly. I heard yelling at my back

to get out as the shelf was coming down on my head and would have crushed me, so I instantly jerked my body back. I just cleared my head by a fraction of a second, and it only missed me by an inch or so—*"phew"*, another close one. See Psalm 23:4 (NIV) and Psalm 34:19–20 (NIV). *"A righteous man may have many troubles, but the Lord delivers him from them all; he protects all his bones, not one will be broken."*

That was enough, so I took a position with the Soil Conservation Department as an assistant involved in research in the use of various compounds to prevent water loss through seepage from farm dams. I eventually tired of the long drive to and from work, so I took another position as a Technical Officer with the Board of Works at the South Eastern Purification Plant complex, a multimillion-dollar expense for the government.

I spent three years working there, and it was an enormous complex with a maze of large underground tunnels where one could drive small electric cars, rather like in the James Bond movies. Security was tight, so when there was an open day, I became one of the security officers. I worked in a laboratory and did many types of analysis work on local samples as well as from samples taken from an outlet for treated water going into Bass Strait. I checked these for heavy metals using a Mass Spectrometer. The Environmental Protection Authority (EPA) requested the results.

My father had a severe car accident at the time, where he nearly died; he could not eat properly after this accident due to having a stroke, and my mother was very worried about him. He told me that when he was exceptionally ill, he could see himself going into a dark tunnel towards a light, but he was told to return when near the light; it was not time for him yet. *This was a near-death experience.*

We decided to have races at the Board of Works, so after running around three miles almost nightly for three months, I felt I ran for Dad's survival after his accident. I entered in an 800 metres race against over thirty men and won a large gold medal. I ran it in close to two minutes. Before the race, we had a betting system up and running, so I put a bet on myself, consequently winning the money. I had been a very fast runner when I was young, being able to run down my opponents when playing rugby.

I owe the glory to God perhaps because I was running for Dad. Some deceitful character stole the real gold medal I had won from its place of display in our laboratory as was requested, so it never found its way to our home.

I had much pain in my left eye caused by the fluores-cent lights at the Board of Works. Fluorescent lights cause this problem in some people. I went to the Eye and Ear Hospital, and they found that my left eye was weak and susceptible to photo-epilepsy, a muscle seizure in the eyes caused by the rapid pulses of artificial light emitted from particular fluorescent tubes. **These weakened my eye so much that I could not even watch a standard colour television for a long time. A local general practitioner prescribed a medicine used as a muscle relaxant to relax the eye muscles. It helped for a while, but after six months, I felt I was getting worse, so I asked the doctor if I could go off the medicine cold turkey, or straight away, and he said, *"Yes"*. This was a no-no, or incorrect advice from him. Anyway, when getting** up the next morning after going off it, I collapsed and only came to when some ambulance men were resuscitating me. I found out later that a number of people had died from the use of this medicine.

My heart was in pain, and I went into a hospital for a check. Over the next month, the withdrawal symptoms were terrible. Again, I could have lost my life, and the left side of my face was partly paralysed for a long time due to a mild stroke from going off the medicine abruptly. Therefore, this could be a warning to be careful with the medicines doctors give, especially on how to wean off them properly. See **Psalm 23:4 (NIV)**, and see **Psalm 34:17–20 (NIV)**.

One night, a neighbour's old wooden house across from our back fence had caught fire and was burning so strongly that our water hoses were useless. Somebody yelled that the power line to the house had fallen on our barbed-wire fence and thus had made the whole fence live. Going immediately into the paddock to see if I could fix anything, I discovered the line had fallen across our paddock. I thought if I picked up the well-insulated line and took it back across the fence carefully, this would make the situation safer. Just as I picked up the line, it started to burn furiously towards me—one big sparkler I can assure you—so quickly that I just managed to drop it by the time it reached me. *"Phew"*, a split second more and that could have been the end of me. It does not pay to play with fireworks, especially live electrical cables. See **Isaiah 43:2 (NIV)**. *"When you pass through the waters, I will be with you; and when you* *pass through the rivers, they will not sweep over you. When you walk through the fire, you will not be burned; the flames will not set you ablaze."*

Later on, another neighbour next to us had gone out and left their oven on, so the kitchen had caught fire. Judy rang the fire brigade as I ran to see if I could do anything. Fortunately, they had left the house unlocked, so I grabbed their hose, ran into the kitchen, and jumped on the kitchen sink. The flames had already burned through the ceiling and into the roof, so I squirted the flames through the hole in the ceiling that had developed and managed to put them out.

However, by this time, the whole kitchen was ablaze and flames surrounded me. It was difficult to breathe, and the heat was becoming unbearable. Realising I had to escape quickly; I jumped down, ran through the flames, and continued to squirt the flames from the other side near the door. Somehow, with the hose, the flames were eventually extinguished, but the whole kitchen was black and ruined; however, I had escaped, just in time. See Isaiah 43:2 (NIV). *"When you pass through the waters, I will be with you; and when you pass through the rivers, they will not sweep over you. When you walk through the fire, you will not be burned; the flames will not set you ablaze."*

Well, the fire fighters arrived and continued to spray the smouldering ruins, which I had already extinguished. I was black from head to toe, covered in soot and some burns, *and guess who received all the thanks in the local paper; not I, anyway, God knows.* When I see how God pulled me out of all these incidents, I realise that He is indeed there with me all along—He is my saviour and my deliverer: **2 Samuel 22:3 (NIV)**—*"my God is my rock, in whom I take refuge, my shield and the horn of my salvation. He is my stronghold, my refuge and my saviour—from violent men you save me."*

During this time Judy gave birth to a baby girl, whom we called Bettina, but complications after childbirth resulted in Judy passing away, a bitter shock to me, as we had been happily married for more than seven years. Going home to an empty house was terrible. I would put on a brave front, but I went home to mourn her loss for a long time. I was very deeply saddened at my loss and wondered when the dark cloud would lift, which took over one-and-a-half years. It was truly sad for her family and me because she was such a pleasant, kind-natured person with a sweet disposition, and my family was very fond of her. I remember going to Wilson's Promontory soon after losing her and looking out to sea with a deep sadness and longing that she would come back to me; it was really an awful experience. One cannot know how awful it is, until it happens to them, to lose the one closest to you, that you dearly love, in the prime of your life.

Back to Melbourne to Live

Running through and from flames when fighting two fires.

Chapter 13

A Miracle Occurs

Bob a good fishing mate, who I had been landscaping with, feeling sorry for me in my loss of Judy, invited me to go to a Charismatic Church and said I should accept Jesus as my saviour and be baptized again. The most important thing I learnt for eternal salvation from condemnation was to sincerely accept Jesus as my saviour through sincere prayer relating to **Romans 10:9 (NIV)**, where it says, *"That if you confess with your mouth, 'Jesus is Lord', and believe in your heart that God raised him from the dead, you will be saved"*. See also **Romans 8:1 (NIV)**: *"Therefore, there is now no condemnation for those who are in Christ Jesus."* In addition, see **2 Corinthians 5:21 (NIV)**: *"God made him who had no sin to be sin for us, so that in him we might become the righteousness of God."* These verses mean that Jesus became our sin on the cross so that we are forgiven through acceptance of Him. We become the righteousness through grace, and there will be no more condemnation for us. Therefore, I learnt that it was very important to say a prayer in relation to Romans 10:9 to avoid condemnation by accepting Jesus as my saviour. I also learnt that one could not get into heaven through good works, no matter how much one has done, even though it is still important to help our fellow man.

I learnt that by doing this, it opened the door to grace through faith, which allows an inheritance of righteousness, health, prosperity, freedom, joy, peace, and forgiveness of sins for us, enabling our freedom through Christ's sacrifice for our redemption, bringing us back into a relationship with God.

I read that God did this for our salvation as He found that humanity could not keep the Law or the Ten Commandments given to them in the Old Testament. See **Romans 8:3 (NIV):** *"For what the law was powerless to do in that it was weakened by the sinful nature, God did by sending his own Son in the likeness of sinful man to be a sin offering. And so he condemned sin in sinful man."* Jesus, the son of God, being a sacrifice, was the solution to this problem.

Through the Holy Spirit, we grow spiritually and have the strength to help avoid future sin. See Romans 8:4. This sacrifice of Jesus also allows the comforter, or Holy Spirit, to work in our lives, empowering us to work much more effectively for the Lord and our fellow man.

After accepting Jesus as my saviour, the **time came for my new baptism, during which the Holy Spirit can come into and work through a person. This involved immersing my whole** body and head underwater in the church. The Holy Spirit can fill one when participating in this, but this Spirit infilling came to me two weeks later; it was a good thing as I was still mourning the loss of Judy.

I was seeking answers to the difficulties and deep sadness I was facing, as nothing else seemed to help, so I picked up a small book about Jesus that belonged to my mother, written back in the 1930s. Although the book was inspiring, I was not reading anything particularly inspiring at the time. Suddenly, I had an extraordinarily powerful tingling feeling going up and down my whole body. I suppose you could call it the living waters, a surprisingly strong and extraordinary feeling, like an electric current, but a very pleasant one. I know God touched me then; He knew I needed His love urgently to help me, so He filled me with the Holy Spirit, as I was seeking sincerely with all my heart for answers. He honoured my search, and He knew my life needed saving; perhaps He was proving His reality and increasing my faith so that I could testify later to the reality of this astounding experience and His powerful unconditional love. See **Romans 5:5 (NIV):** *"And hope does not put us to shame, because God's love has been poured out into our hearts through the Holy Spirit, who has been given to us."* See **Psalm 23:4 (NIV) and Psalm 34:18 (NIV).** *"The Lord is close to the broken-hearted and saves those crushed in spirit."*

When somebody rang the bell in the nursery, I did not want this wonderful feeling to leave me. I had to get up, and when walking out, my body felt very light; I hadn't taken any drugs or alcohol, and as I walked through the darker shade house, I could see a faint blue-white light coming off one of my legs.

After the Holy Spirit infilling, I then approached some people whom I did not know at all with an extraordinarily powerful unconditional love; it was the most wonderful high (or feeling of euphoric love), by far, I have ever experienced. I was so high on this spiritual infilling that I could not function, and as they were looking at me waiting for me to speak, I had to say to the Lord under my breath, "Please let me come down, Lord, so I can sell plants." Then He let me come down to be my old self again.

It was such a pity; I would have loved to be able to hold on to that incredible feeling of euphoric love, His perfect love, and recapture it whenever desired. This feeling was far more powerful than any love you can feel towards another human being, even those madly in love; believe me, because I have been there. *Truly feeling God's unconditional love was so extraordinary, words are not enough to explain it.*

This touch showed me that God was genuine and showed me how extraordinary His unconditional love for us is by revealing Himself in me. It was such an astonishing miracle that I cannot stop talking about it. I felt so privileged that God did this to me, yet humbled. I assure you, I was not dreaming, and was fully conscious of the infilling of the Holy Spirit upon my whole being. **Read 1 Corinthians 2:12 (NIV):** *"We have not received the spirit of the world but the Spirit who is from God, that we may understand what God has freely given us".* In addition, read Galatians

3:26–27 (NIV): *"You are all sons of God through faith in Christ Jesus, for all of you baptized into Christ have clothed yourselves with Christ."*

Sadly, one cannot understand how extraordinary it is until it happens to them. I know the Holy Spirit is always helping me in life as I live with renewed faith in God. This also shows that miracles still happen. Jesus told His disciples to wait until the Holy Spirit came on them before they were His witnesses. **Acts 1:7–8 (NIV):** *"It is not for you to know the times or dates the Father has set by his own authority. But you will receive power when the Holy Spirit comes on you; and you will be my witnesses in Jerusalem, and in all Judea and Samaria, and to the ends of the Earth."* Every time I read this, the Holy Spirit gives me a buzz, to remind me of its truth.

The Holy Spirit would give the disciples power to truly witness and preach to the multitudes, as He also will do for us if we will have faith and try to follow his recommendations. Also, see **Galatians 5:22–23 (NIV):** *"But the fruit of the Spirit is love, joy, peace, patience, kindness, goodness, faithfulness, gentleness and self-control. Against such things there is no law."* Since this infilling, I frequently feel the Holy Spirit, who knows what I am thinking, because when I think of inspiring, positive, especially new ideas or Christian thoughts, I will get a tingling in my head and body. However, when my thoughts are not so positive, nothing happens. *My emotions or brain chemicals do not create these spiritual experiences; I do know the difference.*

This wonderful experience kept me going and gave me hope as I was about to give up. I believe it saved my life, as I found that through this experience of God's unconditional love, I felt I could be healed of my times of mourning and loss. The infilling gave me a new hope, and a desire to study all I could about healing.

I was very excited to find out recently on the Internet on a spiritual experiences site about a woman called Scarlett, who gave a testimony during 2011. She had a very similar experience as myself, especially her explanation of the infilling of the Holy Spirit and God's unconditional love. As He did to me, God directed her to help many people (See Scarlett2, 2011). You will see this in the chapter about being in the right place at the right time; obviously, the Lord led us to these people to help them. My experience was a long time before hers, and this is the first time I have mentioned my experience in any form, except verbally to people. I cannot contain my excitement after reading about this woman's experience, so similar to mine. Her excitement was also so profound in her explanation. This was a baptism of the Holy Spirit, and it has occurred to many others.

I laid hands on people after this with success and renewed faith. A friend in the church told me his brother had only a few weeks to live, as told to him by the doctors in the cancer hospital. *The Holy Spirit compelled me to go and pray over him, so I went in with very strong faith and belief and prayed for his healing. Soon after this, his brother came around to me and said, "John, my brother is healed; he is out of hospital", and he offered me $500, but I said, "No the Lord has done it".*

A Miracle Occurs

This was a genuine touch from God to encourage me to go on in life with a renewed faith, through showing His love to me, so that I could witness to others and pray for the sick. After I had that astounding infilling of the Holy Spirit, I felt I could pray with more faith when I prayed for others and noticed that God had touched them, through their responses, and sensed that there was a spiritual presence with me, although not always noticeable. See **James 5:14–15 (NIV), Psalm 23:4 (NIV),** and **Psalm 34:17–20 (NIV).** In **Mark 16:15–16 (NIV)** it says, *"He said to them, 'Go into all the world and preach the good news to all creation. Whoever believes and is baptized will be saved, but whoever does not believe will be condemned.'"* See also **Mark 16:18 (NIV):** *"They will pick up snakes with their hands; and when they drink deadly poison, it will not hurt them at all; they will place hands on sick people, and they will get well."*

This also reminds me of the time I picked up a large non-poisonous carpet snake in our garage and carried it outside, as I did not fancy having a snake hiding amongst our belongings. It curled itself up, and its huge head was hovering next to mine as if to say, "What do you think you are doing to me?" and he could have easily bitten me, which can still harm, yet he just looked at me as if trusting that I would not hurt him. Yet I do not recommend doing this, as even experts are bitten.

A Miracle Occurs

In my nursery just after a very powerful love infilling, in God's sympathy of the death of my wife, to give me hope.

Chapter 14

My Nursery Business

I kept working at the Board of Works but was not happy there anymore after losing Judy, so I thought about building a plant nursery business to keep my mind occupied. Doing this helped keep my mind busy, although I was still grieving the loss of Judy. I was fortunate that I had a good family, and I was very grateful for their help; they included my mother and father, my sister Catherine and her husband Terry, Donna and Narelle, their daughters, and Diana and Neville, who all helped care for my daughter Bettina. Alan and Betty, who were Judy's mother and father, and Dorothy, Judy's sister, and her husband Norman were a great help also, for which I was very grateful.

I resigned my position as Technical Officer and proceeded to put up a glasshouse, a potting shed, and a shade house area with my father's help. We started to grow plants in six-inch pots, which

I transported to some large outlets with a bread van I had bought. I had to revamp the shelving in the van, so I bought boards made of asbestos, not knowing of the dangers. I asked a neighbour to help me cut them to size with his band saw. We inhaled some dust, and I was coughing blood for a while afterwards and could feel the asbestos splinters in my throat. So far, thank God, I have not developed the deadly disease asbestosis, which has killed many people. See **Psalm 23:4 (NIV)** and **Psalm 34:17–20 (NIV)**.

I eventually decided to get housekeepers in so that Bettina could be at home with me more. Business was going well with the nursery, so I could purchase a nearly new Holden Commodore. I had also put in an automatic irrigation system for the nursery and an orchard of 200 feijoa plants in the remaining land I had. The feijoa's common name is a pineapple guava; it is a delicious fruit native to South America and is tasty once accustomed to, as it is an acquired taste.

Later I decided to propagate Australian native plants and exotics in tubes, so I expanded the nursery and put up four large igloos. At times, I had up to four or five employees, and I often trained young people on work experience. We packed and sent plants nation-wide to all states of Australia and, over the course of ten years or so, sold around half a million or more gums and trees to farmers for windbreaks. I realised recently these would be of great benefit to our world in combating global warming because a tree draws in carbon dioxide during photosynthesis and gives off oxygen for our benefit. The trees tie up the carbon, and in a tree's lifetime, it will draw down many tons of carbon dioxide. This is why it is so important to do extensive tree replacement planting, especially in areas cleared of their forests, create wildlife corridors, use agroforestry, plant windbreaks, and plant shade cover for livestock, increasing farm productivity. We should also care for our natural forests and vegetation around the earth and prevent their destruction, mismanagement, and exploitation. These actions all help to combat global warming.

Exploitation of forests has occurred extensively in the Amazon Basin in South America; this is a disaster as it has promoted global warming, pollution, and erosion. It is necessary to care for our planet by caring for flora and fauna for our future and quality of life on Earth as well as for our children and theirs. God gave us these gifts, and He would desire us to care for them. We are all dependent on each other; therefore, it is necessary for all forms of life on this planet to be kept in balance, for when one disappears, the others will suffer, especially humans. We are actually highly dependent on all other species, plants, and animals, so we need to care for them. See warnings in **Revelation 11:18 (NIV)**, where the Lord says in part, *"for destroying those who destroy the earth"*. This also includes the Earth's inhabitants.

Chapter 15

A Visit to the Philippines

After a few years, I decided to go to the Philippines. I had been writing to a pen pal and decided to meet her. When I was at the Manila airport to get a domestic flight, the ticket officer could not understand my Aussie English; however, the chap next to me could, and he translated what I was saying. I befriended this chap on the flight, and he said his friends were picking him up and would run me into town, so I accepted his offer.

On the way into town, I had a good chat with those in the car, and they said, "Would you like to see some highlights of Davao City?" I agreed, so I spent the next day seeing the popular spots around the town with them. One of these people, who had been in the car with those who drove me into town the previous night, showed interest in me and vice versa; her name was Emelyn. I told her I had to go to meet a pen pal and would come back. I climbed on a bus, which had to travel via an inland route because an earthquake had cut off the regular route to General Santos City.

We had to travel through exceedingly dangerous areas where rebel groups hiding in the mountains were ambushing people and government soldiers. Many white missionaries and foreigners had been captured, held to ransom, and executed in these areas, so it was possible that this could happen to me also. When a group of government soldiers came on board with their machine guns, it made the situation more dangerous for me because of the possibility of ambush. We had to stop at machine-gun posts often along the journey, obviously put there to stop the infiltration of rebels.

In one small town we went through, some children had not seen a white man before, so you can imagine the looks on their faces when they came aboard to look at me. As we were travelling along, I looked back to see my suitcase almost disappearing out of a window; there were no glass windows there, and I grabbed it just in time, "*phew*". The bus was bouncing up and down on the bumps, and these were felt more prominently at the back; a child was laughing as each bump sent me flying so my head nearly hit the roof. I thought, enough, I had better move forward in the bus. The driver was worried and drove frantically all the way, nearly rolling the bus off the side of the road as a horse and cart passed on the opposite side.

After I arrived, dusty and rather exhausted, my pen pal's mother offered me a balut, a chicken still in the egg, and when I saw its poor little head, I nearly vomited and politely said, no thank you; they eat them as an energizer. After chatting awhile, I went with my pen pal on a motorbike to the sea where they were having a mass baptism for many people. During the evening, she said she would marry me if I sent money to her parents and only if I joined her church, I had not even proposed. I felt in a way she wanted me just for my money, and it put me off, so I went back to the girl I had met in Davao. She was rather cute, and there was some chemistry. I spent more time in Davao, and we decided we would like to marry. I must admit now that I was naïve and should have got to know her for much longer rather than deciding so early. Anyway, we went to Manila together to process papers for her to come to Australia.

After doing this, she went home, and I went on to Baguio City, where I went to some faith healers for healing of the slightly paralysed left side of my face, which occurred when going off a medicine, which I mentioned earlier. Their healing techniques did not seem to help, but another well-respected and revered healer, only asked for a donation in aid of building a church. I also remember having a greater faith in God healing me perhaps because of what I had heard about her success with God working through her.

When I left her healing session, I could feel the warmth and circulation flowing through that numbed area of my face for the first time. I knew then that God honoured her work, because of her sincere purpose in desiring to build a church and so God had performed a *real miracle healing* in me—how wonderful God is. Read **Acts 19:11–12 (NIV):** *"God did extraordinary miracles through Paul, so that even handkerchiefs and aprons that had touched him were taken to the sick, and their illnesses were cured and the evil spirits left them."*

After that, I was happy that the paralysed feeling in the side of my face had gone, and it never came back again. I then went back to Davao, where I married Emelyn. I had to come back to Australia as my visa was running out, so I couldn't spend enough time with her, and she had to stay in Davao until all her papers were processed. After a few months, she arrived in Australia.

I soon discovered she was unstable. I had not seen this instability in the Philippines as my time with her was short and she had managed to cover it up. She was manic-depressive, also called bipolar disorder. Later her family apologized to me for not telling me about her illness and thanked me for trying to help her; however, I thought it unfair they had not told me about her problem earlier.

The situation I was now in was quite a shock and concern for me. Anyway, I decided to persevere and put up with the entire goings-on, but it stressed me intensely. I thought having a child (a little boy called Glen) might help her settle down, but it didn't. One minute she would be fine or happy and the next minute for no reason would go crazy; this was one of the symptoms of the illness. Often, times together were pleasant, and she loved me, but many bad things happened; however, I do not wish to run her down or talk about the ordeals I went through. She could not help her illness, so I forgave her. Therefore, this was a big lesson for me to know one's future partner better than I had, as I suffered from much stress and trauma from her for many years because of this mistake.

One day she cooked with a frypan and it caught fire, so I tried to carry it outside; however, it exploded over my arm, so my whole arm was covered in oil on fire. I reached the laundry basin and fortunately got my arm under cold water; however, the pain was unbearable, and I went to hospital, where they had to operate and cut all the skin off my arm. It looked like a leg of lamb in a butcher's shop, not like an arm at all. It finally, miraculously, healed back to usual after a long time. Anyway, I do not blame her as it could have happened with anybody.

On a more pleasant note, after having a tooth extracted and the dentist not getting the entire tooth out, we nevertheless packed the car and went to Sheep Yard Flat at the foot of Mount Buller to look for some deer together. We put up the tent before hunting and set off up the foothills. She had brought a thermometer. I had a hunting bow and a .30-30 rifle; I was looking for Sambar deer, and we climbed one ridge and decided to head back down as it was getting late. However, we crossed one gully and went down but could not find the tent. Emelyn was walking slowly, and by now, it had become dark—so dark that we could not find our way through another gully to find the tent.

Therefore, we realised we would have to spend the night out in the open. Fortunately, I had brought matches again. In addition, I had brought a packet of aspirin tablets, fortunately, as my mouth started to agonize in pain with an infection from the broken tooth for which I had to take at least three tablets to dampen the pain. We found some dry logs on a ridge, but the wind was truly icy, so we tried to make a branch hut running off the logs and then light a fire. This worked for a while until it got colder, so during the night, we had to abandon the

branch shelter, as our heads and backs were freezing. We had to build two more fires around us to survive. Where our heads and feet stuck out in the cold was agony, and we took turns in keeping the fires going.

This saved our lives as the temperature dropped to minus 10 degrees or lower. If I had not had the matches, we would have lost our lives that night—saved by God again. Psalm 34:17–20 (NIV) and Psalm 25:15 (NIV): *"My eyes are ever on the Lord, for only he will release my feet from the snare."* In addition, Psalm 23:1–4 (NIV): *"The Lord is my Shepherd; I shall not be in want. He makes me lie down in green pastures, he leads me beside the quiet waters, He restores my soul. He guides me in paths of righteousness for his name's sake. Even though I walk through the valley of the shadow of death, I will fear no evil, for you are with me; your rod and your staff, they comfort me."* This is a famous verse from the Bible used by people in times of trouble and was a favourite of my mother's also. I recited the latter verse rather anxiously once; when battling in my canoe against a powerful wind; only just making it to shore, with total exhaustion; when on another camping trip with Emelyn, see **Psalm 23:4 (NIV)** and **Psalm 34:17–20 (NIV)**.

We found our way back in the morning and quickly packed and headed back to Melbourne, where I had to go on antibiotics immediately for my gum infection. Although the environment was freezing, she was a good and helpful partner then, but the frustrating and sad fact about her illness was the changes it would create in her, which were out of her control. It was a pity, I could not take it anymore, as sometimes she would argue all night until I

A Visit to the Philippines

could not speak, and my heart was hurting. She would smash things and even try to jump out of the car through none of my doing—I had not provoked her in any way. These actions were the result of her illness, and her family told me later that she was doing these things in the Philippines before I had even met her.

After four years of marriage, I could not take the stress she was causing me anymore; she had already been in hospital twice for her manic depression with breakdowns, despite my trying in every way to help her, but what could I do if she would not take her medicine? After a stressful time with her, I went away camping with a friend, Steve, so I could decide what to do. I was only around 34 and was diagnosed with high blood pressure from the stress. I realised I would have to divorce her or the stress would finish me. I had to take Betaloc, a blood pressure medicine, and have had high blood pressure ever since, so deciding to send her back to the Philippines with Glen was the best option.

She would not leave without Glen, so it was a very difficult decision to make, as I would miss my little boy. I felt this was the best decision I could make; however, she did not want to leave me and was upset. If we separated in Australia, she would not cope, and it was better for her to stay with her sister in the Philippines, where I knew they would be taken care of. I decided I would go and see them sometimes. So when they were about to depart, I felt upset, especially letting my boy go, but I realised I had to decide. I already had Bettina, and I could have kept Glen also, because of her illness, but if I kept both, I felt it would be unfair to her, and make my situation worse.

Chapter 16

Single Again

After she left, an enormous weight and burden lifted from my shoulders and mind. I kept my mind busy with my nursery and had to find housekeepers to help look after my daughter again. I managed to get away on a cruise on the ship "Fairstar" for ten days to the South Pacific islands, namely, Tonga, Noumea, Fiji, Rarotonga, and Western Samoa. I made friends on board, and we had a wonderful time. When we visited a resort in Noumea, the guard spoke in French, and everyone looked puzzled; however, I remembered a few words of French, so he allowed us in. The beach was much like Port Phillip Bay. At night, island dancers entertained us before we boarded the ship again.

In Tonga, we had a magnificent feast on the beach near some caves, where the islanders performed fire dancing and singing and showed much friendliness and kindness; they even appeared sad when we left. Our visit to Western Samoa was special also, where they performed the entire range of Pacific Island dances, including those of the Maoris from New Zealand. We were invited to go and dance with them...good fun. We also saw the home of Robert Louis Stevenson, the writer of the famous book *Robinson Crusoe*. We travelled by bus, listening to marvellous island music, and spent some hours swimming at one of the beaches, where I was surprised to meet some of my sister Diana's friends, who were on the same cruise.

I was also fortunate enough to get away to Bali for seven days or so at a different time. It was a wonderful experience, as I met people from many countries and did some sightseeing with them. One was a professional photographer I befriended from Reykjavik in Iceland, and as I had just gained my motorbike licence, we decided to explore the island on the bike. At one stage, I was going uphill on a dirt road and the bike was slowing, so I decided to accelerate a little. **The front of the bike went up in the air, and we were thrown off over the cliff, but strangely, we did not have a scratch between us; yet it was a lesson learned. See Psalm 23:4 (NIV)** and **Psalm 34:17–20 (NIV).**

We had an enjoyable time. She would say, "Stop the bike," so I did, and she photographed children playing under the palms and poor old turtles in their cages ready for market. Turtle steaks were on the menu there in the restaurants. We stopped by ancient temples covered in intricate carvings depicting life in times gone by. People are very clever even nowadays in wood and stone carving in these countries. During one of the nights in Bali, we went out to the club that was more recently destroyed by a bomb, killing more than 200 people—a shocking event in Australian history and a night where I am pleased that I was not there.

Life was easier again, thank goodness, but I still had stress problems from the marriage I previously discussed, and I still felt traumatized from it. Later after many past dramas, and a serious car accident; I was diagnosed with Post-traumatic Stress Disorder (PTSD); which brings many strong normal people to their knees; including soldiers, policemen; those in serious accidents; and the physically or emotionally abused. Despite my efforts to resolve, I found I was easily stressed and had much trouble sleeping, a condition that was non-existent when I was younger. Although, I claimed God's healing and I believe I would be far worse without God's help, as faith and confidence in God helps to maintain peace of mind.

I had met a few Australian women over time and was going with one, who I was not sure about, so I eventually broke off with her. I decided to write to Filipino women again, as I knew I had been unlucky and there were many good ones. I wrote to a lady called Norma, who seemed pleasant in her photograph and letters, and she was a wonderful Christian lady of whom I became fond. As a pastor's daughter, she grew up in a Christian environment. In her teenage life, she was deeply involved in church activities as a Sunday school teacher, choir director, and youth leader and served in the management team and Church Board. She also finished a University degree in Business Management and Accounting.

She was working in two Christian corporations, the CCF Inc. and the Asia-Pacific Nazarene Theological Seminary Inc. in Manila. We were writing for almost two years until we decided to meet in the Philippines. After meeting, Norma and I became engaged, and she showed me some of the Visayas region of Cebu. We stayed on Mactan Island, where Ferdinand Magellan died in a battle with Lapu-Lapu in 1521, a Philippine hero. Eventually the Spanish ruled the Philippines for centuries.

On arriving back in Manila before leaving, we started processing Norma's paperwork to come to Australia on a fiancé visa. I was back in Melbourne attending my nursery business and looking after Bettina while waiting for Norma. When I rang Norma, I asked her to speak to Mum, and they became fond of each other, often writing to one another, Norma still has the letters. Several months after this, Mum developed a brain tumour and could not speak, so it was a difficult time for me.

Dad was in New Zealand getting a metal hip replacement, and I know Mum was worried about him. Mum had been an excellent help in caring for my daughter, Bettina, when I needed help, so I was very grateful for this and took her to church, trying to be always there for her as a son, and friend, in her difficult times. Helping me was never a burden to Mum but one that she enjoyed.

We learned Mum had an incurable tumour on the brain. She was admitted to hospital where she stayed for almost two months, and our cousin Wilma, a nurse, did a wonderful job caring for her. We had spent many happy times on their dairy farm with John, Wilma, and their children, Andrea, Jacqueline, Karen, and Matthew, all wonderful Christians. I told Mum to hold on as Norma was coming to Australia, and hold on she did. Norma finally arrived, and I took her straight to the hospital where Mum was. She held Mum's hand and prayed a wonderful prayer for her. Although Mum had not spoken or moved her arms and body for almost a month, following Norma's prayer, she opened her eyes and lifted her arms to Norma. God gave her strength; it was astonishing.

Read **Isaiah 41:10 (NIV):** *"So do not fear, for I am with you; do not be dismayed, for I am your God. I will strengthen you and help you; I will uphold you with my right hand."* I told Mum I loved her, and she put her hand over her heart for Norma and me. The following day she died. God, knowing Mum's desire to meet Norma, had kept her alive, as it was important for Mum to meet Bettina's new mother so her heart would be at ease about Bettina; how wonderful God is for us. Norma was well organized, a wonderful person whom I loved, and she provided strength and ongoing support in my life, which I needed to keep going after all the trials I had faced.

Chapter 17

I Marry Again

I had to marry Norma soon after she arrived, as required for those on a fiancé visa, and as it was shortly after Mum had died, it was a difficult time for us all. It was especially difficult to be jovial, although I was happy about marrying Norma. We went for our honeymoon in South Australia and stayed with Norma's nice cousin Judith and her husband Alan, who ran a furniture business at the time.

We continued growing plants in tubes in the plant nursery. Competition was high, as two other tube grower nurseries had started up in our street, one owner having mechanized seedling-transplanting equipment so that he could turn them out much faster and at a lower cost.

As our income started to ease off, I took another position with Jennings as a Certificated Gardener for three years, where I was in a maintenance team, caring for more than twenty acres of business parks and gardens with another gardener called Peter.

Norma continued to run the nursery and sell off our last plants during the second year of my work at Jennings. As I was working long hours and nearly all weekend, including mowing my orchard, chopping wood, taking care of the nursery, and property maintenance, it was getting tiring for me. However, I kept growing the 200 trees in the feijoa orchard, and eventually, after nearly five years, they began to bear fruit—large, juicy, green, egg-shaped fruit—and they were delicious. The seedlings I had budded with Mammoth and Triumph varieties, which came from Scoresby Horticultural Research Station.

Norma and I joined a church in Frankston and enjoyed the services and a fellowship group, where I completed a "Certificate in Discipleship" so I could help newcomers and those who had accepted Jesus as their saviour. I went away camping with the men's group from the church, near a mountain river. As there were many of us, I used one of their chainsaws so they could gather plenty of timber for firewood, as it was quite chilly. We did some wild water kayaking in the river, all of us having to wear wet suits. On one particular rapid, two of the men came out, and their kayak jammed itself between underwater rocks; it was never recovered, but luckily, they were okay. We were winning the race until we came out on the last rapids…anyway it was great fun.

Chapter 18

A Disastrous Fishing Trip

One evening I invited a friend named Ray out snapper fishing. He was married to a Filipino woman named Lena with whom we used to have parties. I had bought a Bond-wood boat, which had a light fiberglass coating for protection. We set off in the evening from Frankston, and after travelling several kilometres in the dark, we hit something, later learning there were logs in the bay. It cracked the hull for about one metre on each side, and water started coming in. We were already about three miles out from the shore, and the offshore wind was increasing. Ray said he could not swim, to my surprise, and he was already in his 50s. I had installed a water pump, which worked at home but did not out there. I asked Ray to put on a life jacket and to start bailing.

I then gave a Pan-Pan radio call for help, and explained our problems. They told me to start the motor and head for shore, which I did; they were busy with another boat in distress but kept in touch.

My boat was taking water much faster than we could bail, so I searched for the flares; fortunately, I had studied up on emergency procedures prior to this.

The motor suddenly stopped, as it was swamped, so I took time off to PRAY, as our lives were genuinely at risk. We were miles out at sea, in dark conditions, and the waves were nearly one metre high, so they knocked the boat sideways. We were in a very dangerous and grave situation as there were no rescue boats in sight. I gave the coastguard a compass bearing and approximate position off Oliver's Hill and told them I would set off a flare; however, nobody saw it or reported it to the police, and by this time, the boat was about to sink.

Rapidly grabbing the other flare, I set it off just before my boat sank. About two seconds after it went off, the boat disappeared from under our feet—"*phew*", just in time.

We were in the depths with waves going over our heads. A woman on Oliver's Hill saw the flare and rang the police fortunately, and another large launch coming back from Mornington had seen it, luckily for us. They later told us they were going to stay the night there but said it was getting too rough, so they were coming back to Patterson River. I had checked the weather forecast before going out, as I always did; however, an offshore wind had developed, so one can never be too careful.

Meanwhile, while in the sea, Ray panicked and grabbed me around the neck (typical of what happens when one panics). I told him all was okay; I kept cool all the time. I was too busy saving our lives, and fortunately, I could swim well. I dragged Ray to the bow of the boat, still pointing skyward because of an air compartment up front that was keeping the boat buoyant. We held on for what seemed an eternity and were becoming cold, as hypothermia can kill people quickly depending on the water temperature. Out of the darkness, like a ghost, came this enormous launch—what a wonderful sight and relief for us.

They pulled up beside us, but Ray panicked again and, while climbing aboard the boat, ripped his leg open with much blood loss. I hoped there were not any sharks around, as I was still in the water. All my fishing gear, toolbox, and equipment had disappeared out of the boat, and the anchor had fallen out, anchoring it to the bottom.

We tied a thick, new white rope to the bow of my boat, as I asked them to try to tow it, but the rope snapped, so they were not too amused. However, the Lord saved us; *Ray commented later, and mind you, he was a nonbeliever,* **"That prayer you said, John, saved our lives."** Read **Isaiah 58:9 (NIV)**: *"Then you will call and the LORD will answer; you will cry for help, and he will say: Here am I. If you do away with the yoke of oppression, with the pointing finger and malicious talk."* In addition, read **Psalm 18:6 (NIV)**, and read **Isaiah 43:2 (NIV)**. *"When you pass through the waters, I will be with you; and when you pass through the rivers, they will not sweep over you. When you walk through the fire, you will not be burned; the flames will not set you ablaze."* I was very grateful to the Lord.

Sometimes people have to go through extreme trauma like this before they come to God…what a pity, but better than not at all. We went back to Patterson River where we met the police, who took us back to my car in Frankston.

We were in a state of shock to a degree, especially Ray; he had turned a blue-purple colour and nearly died, and it took him months to get over this experience, but he thanked me for keeping cool and saving his life.

I asked my niece Donna's husband Richard the next day to help me retrieve my boat, which I had put a compass bearing on when it sank so that we could find it. If not retrieved the next day, the police were going to sink it, as it was a water hazard. Richard's boat was a Haines Hunter with a good-sized motor, undoubtedly needed, as my boat was a dead weight full of water.

I had to swim again to my boat to tie a rope to it, and as I did, a rope tangled around my body. Strangely, but suddenly, much air started to escape from the bow, and I thought it might sink. I quickly untangled the rope around my body, as it would have taken me down with it if it did sink. We slowly towed the boat ashore and winched it onto a boat trailer, but as it was so heavy from being full of water, the winch's link straightened just as we got it secured.

I took it immediately to a boat mechanic and asked him to save the motor and get it going before rust set in. Although it had been under the sea for about twelve hours, get it going he did—how astonishing. I then took the boat back to Catherine and Terry's place where Dad saw it, and I noticed tears in his eyes, as he must have realised how fortunate I was to be alive.

A Disastrous Fishing Trip

If I had not studied how to use the radio, flares, and safety procedures, as well as keeping calm, we could have lost our lives, but I give the glory to God, as ultimately He heard my prayers and guides us in all our ways.

Read **Psalm 23:4 (NIV)** and **Psalm 34:17–20 (NIV)**. Many men had lost their lives in their boats on Port Phillip Bay. This did not put me off boating, so I bought another, better fibreglass boat, as I enjoyed going out. As the saying goes, I am a tiger for punishment, am I not?

One day a friend, Ron, asked if I would take him out fishing, to which I agreed. Well, he was a large chap, and as we went out, my fifteen-foot half cabin boat was leaning to one side with his weight. After arriving and throwing out some lines, it became a little choppy, not much mind you; however, the poor chap got seasick and was vomiting over the side. I was concerned as when he leaned over, so did the boat, and I was worried if he became fatigued he might fall out, and heaven help me if I had to fish him out of the sea. Can you imagine the angle of the boat? Not wanting to go all the way back yet as we wanted to catch some fish, I decided to put a life jacket on him only to discover he was so wide around the tummy area that the jackets could not be fastened.

As he was feeling worse, I thought I had better take him in for safety. When we arrived, he was so exhausted that he could not get out of the boat, and I felt my muscles were not big enough to lift him. I prayed for help. Then miraculously, just when shackling the boat to my car, a truck pulled alongside us, launching another boat. Well, you would not believe it, but there were three strong men in that truck, so with the four of us, we managed to lift him onto the back of their truck and finally onto the ground. Another miracle I thought, as otherwise I could have had a very sore back and arms for a long time had I tried to lift him myself. So there you are, God is with us in the funny times and the bad times (not so funny for this poor guy though), and this story shows the power of prayer, as you will also see later in the book. See **Psalm 40:1–3 (NIV)**: *"I waited patiently for the Lord: he turned to me and heard my cry. He lifted me out of the slimy pit, out of the mud and mire; he set my feet on a rock and gave me a firm place to stand. He put a new song in my mouth, a hymn of praise to our God."* Sounds familiar doesn't it; and reminds me about a return trip to French Island; Norma, I, and a very worried pilot took, in a light plane; which battled against quite a violent wind, making hardly any headway, wings shaking alarmingly, thinking they might fall off; but again the Lord heard our prayers, see **Psalm 23:4 (NIV)** and **Psalm 34:17–20 (NIV)**.

A Disastrous Fishing Trip

Rescuing my sunken boat the following day.

Chapter 19

Our Children

When I decided to close the nursery, it had operated for more than 10 years. Norma took a position near where I was working, so I dropped her off and picked her up after work. In winter, we were leaving in the dark in the morning and getting home after dark. Norma lost her first child prematurely, which upset her, naturally, but shortly after was expecting another, born in August, and we named him Jonathan.

During his birth, Norma had to undergo an emergency operation, as this was a dangerous situation where Norma could have lost her life, thank-you God again for saving her. **Psalm 23:4 (NIV) and Psalm 34:17–20 (NIV).**

Jonathan was such a cute child and was such a joy for us. Norma was a good mother and loved caring for him. He was exceedingly intelligent and could already operate our VHS player and play the piano delightfully by the age of two. Who was guiding his little fingers I wonder, can you imagine? He had not yet been taught to play. His tiny fingers played so gently and exquisitely what seemed genuine tunes, entirely harmonious, and he would look up at us and smile for approval as he played; it was extraordinary. Was this a little mature spirit playing in him, or was he a genius or both? (He should have continued his future piano lessons.) I wish I had taken a movie of him.

He loved pushing his little cart and helping pick up feijoas in the orchard; he was a genuine blessing and joy for Norma and me. Later at high school, he became Dux in year eight (top for all year 8 students) in the high school. While at school, he joined the Australian Air Force Cadets and was one of the outstanding cadet officers, out of six, to represent Australia with a scholarship in the International Air Cadet Exchange to Canada with other worldwide cadet officers.

They went to Montreal, Vancouver, Quebec, Ontario, and the Niagara Falls. He led his squadron in all Anzac parades wearing his grandfather's medals and was standing next to the Mayor in a picture on the front page of the local newspaper. We were exceedingly proud of him, as he was so smart marching like his grandfather, Major Douglas Coleman. He later achieved honours in a Bachelor Degree in Multimedia, also becoming privileged to be a Golden Key International Honours Society member, and achieved the Griffith Award for Academic Excellence for studies in a Masters of Digital Design degree.

When still at university, he worked as an Art Director. Currently, he has already worked successfully for two companies in multimedia software development. He is currently an Innovation team lead in Multimedia as well as in app project management and online technology consultation. This job takes him to different countries, such as New Zealand, Hawaii, Bali, India, and the Philippines, for business conferences. He is also building WordPress websites for businesses as a sideline business. I help him with the search-engine optimisation (SEO). He is also a youth leader in a large church, so is busy, having just come back from an interesting trip to Peru with friends, an eye opener for him with such a unique culture.

Bettina is a lovely person, and although it was unfortunate that her maternal mother passed away, she was lucky that she had much care and love from all the family, and we all love her very much. She is very kind and thoughtful and helped us care for Jonathan when he was small. When she had dancing lessons, in which she excelled, she won several dancing prizes. Bettina's cousin Kelly (Diana's daughter) was in the same dancing class.

Bettina was also in the *Wizard of Oz* play, a high school production at a community theatre, and played a principal vocal part as Glinda in the preview and matinees as well as one of the Oz people at night and as a munchkin once. She was, and still is, a talented singer, as she sings solo for a church. She currently does hospital work and has qualifications in marketing. She was involved in child-care work for a long time, and I remember one day when I picked her up, the excited children she cared for surrounded her, as they just loved her, and waved her goodbye as she left.

Glen is a pleasant, intelligent, and unassuming chap, able to speak three languages. He wanted to come back to Australia, so we brought him back here when he was eighteen to live with us. He sings and plays the guitar well and is keen on physics, science, and Christianity as well as the unknown phenomena; he is rather like me in the things he likes. He is presently enjoying a course in Laboratory Technology. He desires to further his studies towards achieving more qualifications in science. He also has a pretty daughter called Rania. Rania's mother, Rigbe, is a lovely, caring person. Fortunately, our children are all Christians, and we love them all.

Glen and Bettina, when young, would often go and play with my sister Diana's and Neville's children, Kelly and Sam, children of a similar age. Kelly and Sam travelled around the world, working as they went, and are both good teachers in different fields. They are doing well in their lives.

Chapter 20

In the Right Place to Help Others

I reflect on the many times I seemed to be in the right place just at the time people needed help, which has happened so many times that I find it astounding. When in Griffith, living on an orchard, I heard a woman screaming and ran out to find her being attacked by a large dog, so yours truly saved the day for her.

Another time Norma and our children went camping on the Murray River. Nearby a group of young people were camping. Another group was directly across the river from them. During the night, they started drinking alcohol and shouting back and forth to each other across the river, which was in flood at the time. Eventually, as one group had a dingy, they thought they would all get together.

The group on the other side brought their boat across, picked up as many as they could fit in the boat, and rowed back. Halfway across, the boat capsized, and it was everyone for themselves in a flooded Murray River at night. They were all washed downstream quickly, some screaming for help, some hardly able to swim, yet somehow they managed to reach shore, thank God. We could hear panic-stricken teenagers coming back, so I grabbed a bottle of rescue remedy from our camp, as I had studied about and knew the value of natural remedies, especially through experience.

Many were upset and screaming when they got back, especially the girls. I gave them some rescue remedy drops, and within seconds, they were all quiet. *"What was that?"* they said. I said that it was rescue remedy, especially for emergencies and shock; it is safe and given to distressed people, babies, animals, and birds, having helped thousands of people. See Psalm 23:4 (NIV) and Psalm 34:17–20 (NIV).

Rescue remedy is one of the Bach remedies made originally from the dew off natural herbs and flowers. It is one of God's remedies, like many other natural remedies, that He provides through nature. God has given us many varieties of plants for food and medicine, and millions of people around the world still rely heavily on plants for their medicines. Australia now has its own range made from native plants.

When I have been out walking, I seem to find people in need often. I saw a chap fall from the back of his boat parked at a jetty while the outboard motor was still running, and his wife was screaming for help, as he was right next to the motor, so I ran down and grabbed his arm and pulled him onto the jetty away from the motor. He was so close I thought the propeller could finish him. The boat was still in drive but had just been fastened to the jetty.

Another time in the same area, a woman was in a predicament with a full shopping trolley on a sloped jetty trying to open a locked gate; she could not get the gate open and was close to losing the trolley. I happened to be there just at the right time to help her.

When fishing Westernport Bay from my boat, I received an emergency Pan-Pan call on my basic only 27 MHz marine radio from a distressed yachtsman, who said he was just off the coast of Tasmania and in severe trouble. The radio I had is only supposed to have a 10 to 15 nautical mile range in the line of sight, yet I picked up this man's distress call around 400 kilometres away. Who else could have carried his call of distress to my radio over that long distance? Surely only God, as I must have been the only one on duty at the time, despite being well out of range of his call for help. I immediately contacted the local coastguard, and they reached their Tasmanian counterpart, having more sophisticated equipment than I did, and thus were able to save him. Shortly afterwards they thanked and reassured me that they could send help to that man in distress.

One particular day I could see an enormous shark with our fish finder, swimming under the boat; if you think I was thinking about "Jaws", you are right. It was longer than my boat, which was 15 feet long. This was near Seals Rock, where there were many seals, on the southern end of Phillip Island. This was a renowned area for the biggest white pointer sharks. They grow so big by feeding on the seals. When we turned around to head back, I asked my friend to take the wheel at steering for a while so that I could troll for fish, and a huge wave came up behind us. He did not know what to do, so my quick, evasive action on the steering and throttle saved the day, as we did not fancy providing a change in menu for that shark.

God uses a man or woman to save or help others, and these are only a few of many events like this. It is truly astonishing how the Lord uses one to help others. See **Psalm 23:4 (NIV)** and **Psalm 34:17–20 (NIV)**. See **Isaiah 58–9 (NIV)** and **Psalm 18:6 (NIV)**. *"In my distress I called to the LORD; I cried to my God for help. From his temple he heard my voice; my cry came before him, into his ears."*

Chapter 21

Some Dangerous Journeys

After deciding to have a holiday break from Melbourne for ten days or so, we drove to Queensland, as far as Rainbow Beach near Gympie. On the way back, we visited Macleay Island, where my family and I had bought a block of land between us, so obviously I wanted to see it. We camped out on the block; however, mosquitoes attacked us that night despite having mosquito-repellent to spray. Despite this, we fell in love with the island and found a block looking over the sea. It was delightful, so we decided to put a deposit on it to purchase.

On the way home, as we were coming close to a town called Parkes early in the morning, Norma was driving to give me a break, and suddenly I heard Norma gasp with fright, as a car came out to pass a semitrailer—it was heading straight at us. A surge of adrenaline bolted me into action; I grabbed

the steering wheel, pulling it down to avoid a head-on collision between both cars travelling at a fair speed towards each other.

Norma had frozen with fear, so I just got our car out of the other's path with a fraction of a second to spare. It missed us by inches, and our car went right off the side of the road to avoid the collision. If there had been trees in our way, which there typically are toward Parkes that would have been the end also, so thank God again for saving us. Psalm 23:4 (NIV) and Psalm 34:19–20 (NIV). *"A righteous man may have many troubles, but the Lord delivers him from them all; he protects all his bones, not one will be broken."*

One day when going to work on a foggy, rainy day, I was coming up a hill on a freeway travelling at a safe speed, and there in front of me, just over the hill, was a car in my lane. He was in the middle of the freeway, not moving and with no warning lights on—what a surprise. I looked for evasive action; however, there were cars on either side of mine, so I could not cross lanes, and if I did, the car could have gone sideways because of the wet conditions, which could have created a worse accident. I quickly decided to brake as much as possible, although not too hard, as that could have caused the car to go sideways also.

All these decisions were required instantaneously, and sadly, the only option I had was to run into the back of him at a reduced speed, despite my having an excellent driving record. This person had not put his warning lights on, which he should have. He was young, and I learned that he had only recently received his licence. The best driver could not have avoided this collision.

My car hit his so that his car was written off up to the front doors. The car engine had turned sideways, and the collision was severe enough that my seat belt nearly snapped, and I had bad whiplash to my neck, in which I still have trouble. His car careered off the road. Fortunately, the police arrived, and after an explanation, they were annoyed with him, not me. Luckily, the comprehensive insurance covered it for both cars. Anyway, again I thank the Lord for saving my life; see Psalm 23:4 (NIV) and Psalm 34:17–20 (NIV).

After this accident, swimming in heated pools helped my neck, but I felt shocked for a while after this. I had this phobia of driving into the back of cars when driving close to them, but after perseverance, the shock and phobia diminished as I regained my driving confidence.

Soon after this, a large tree had fallen in a storm where I worked, so we chopped it up for removal. However, its large rootball was embedded in the ground, so we had to chop the roots and clear soil from beneath to drag it out with a tractor. I was in the trench behind it when it fell back on me. Despite having a rope tied firmly to the tractor, it dragged the tractor back and pinned me to the ground. My co-worker, Peter, jumped frantically on the tractor and gradually dragged the tree stump off my body. This was not a very nice experience.

I also found that I had to sit down all the time; my energy would only last for five minutes, and my head was shaking at one stage as though I had malaria. I could not figure out what was wrong; I went to the doctor and told them about the fatigue, but they did not even give me a blood test to discover what it was. I battled on; it was a terrible fatigue, and none of us knew what was wrong with me. Later a blood test revealed it was Ross River Virus, similar to malaria, from when we were camping on the island, giving me Chronic Fatigue Syndrome (CFS). Sometimes I was not so fatigued; however, it would come back again and hit me like a ton of bricks. Malaria can do this also.

Much of our work apart from ride-on mowing and garden care was hand mowing steep drains along the highways and sides of buildings for lengthy periods, and with the CFS, this was becoming a nightmare, as I was almost collapsing. One day I felt so ill I had to lie down in the shed, not knowing what was wrong, not having been diagnosed with the virus then. We had eighteen year olds for training sometimes, and when they did these jobs, we would find them cowering under bushes, and they would say, "Oh, it's too difficult!" I was doing these jobs all the time.

Chapter 22

Our Move to Macleay Island

We decided the only answer was to move to Macleay Island to try to recover. The Ross River Virus, a nasty infection, had killed a number of people, including a young swimming instructor. I later learned from a specialist that an infection or poison in the system combined with previous severe stress and trauma, which I had had, could produce Chronic Fatigue Syndrome (CFS). The illness was considered far more severe than fibromyalgia with which I have seen even young people in wheelchairs; one I knew was happy and healthy before coming down with this. The doctor believed the sprays I had used and the crop duster plane experience added to this problem, as I was still having milder fatigue problems before getting Ross River Virus. I was also feeling the cold intensely, and dampness from water lying under our house was adding to muscle aches and pains, which made us decide to sell up and leave, as there was no other option.

The CFS known symptoms were headaches, fever, pain in the joints, easily becoming stressed, anxiety, slow thinking, and temporary inability to think because of energy cuts and circulation cuts of up to twenty per cent, plus insomnia apart from the terrible fatigue where I could hardly stand.

We eventually sold our property by auction but did not receive our desired amount, and after a large tidy up and packing sessions, where our possessions filled half a semitrailer, we finally headed for Brisbane. We made our base in Kingston, where I got quotes to build on our block on the island. Our builder from the mainland managed to get his contractors to camp on the block while they were building, and, finally, after around nine months and close to Christmas, our house was finished. I decided to get a friend, Kevin, a painter on the island, to help finish it.

The house was on a delightful spot looking over the Bay. The Bay with all its moods in changeable weather was so interesting, especially with waves rolling in, which would lull us to sleep. Sometimes the sea was calm and presented reflections of the mangroves in the morning, and there were delightful sunsets at sundown. The parrots and many species of birds would welcome the sunrise with joyful songs; it was such a delightful place—quite spiritual at times I felt.

God's creations were such an inspiration there, and we made friends with a number of people. This was a good time to try to recover, and it was only when we moved to the island that they discovered I had Ross River Virus; I had picked it up there from the mosquitoes when camping out, before going back to Melbourne. A specialist diagnosed me with Chronic Fatigue Syndrome, and with the PTSD I thought, what a great combo, no wonder I was battling. I found out that the CFS and PTSD make one easily susceptible to anxiety and stress, and eventually remedies for these helped ease the symptoms; however, they slowed me down to a degree, which was annoying at times.

Waking to the sounds of the seaside and parrots in the surrounding gum trees helped lift my spirits somewhat, so I felt there must be a purpose in all this. I did much soul searching, trying to plan ways to use my time wisely. I went to the doctors many times to try various medicines, and it was very difficult and time consuming trying to find the right ones, as they had so many side effects. I investigated natural remedies that might help and, in the process, became knowledgeable about herbs, vitamins, and homeopathic remedies, some of which were able to help to a degree to alleviate some symptoms.

Despite my efforts, the problems kept returning, and I tried doing some part-time work but found that I could hardly stand up, much less work with energy. I heard that long-lasting fatigue could be a lifetime problem for some, and some people were in wheelchairs with it, some not able to get out of bed for months. I found it impossible to get back that stamina we need sometimes, and this was annoying. I finally had to accept my lot but was determined not to give up.

I often wondered what this burden meant; *perhaps it was so I would pursue my painting talent, or perhaps so that I would need to rely on God so that I could later testify to His greatness as I am now doing, or perhaps both to help others. Therefore, here is an example where God can turn difficulties into blessings.* I battled on, but it was difficult. In the past, I could forget myself and become entirely engrossed spiritually with my painting, as many artists do, and this is the most rewarding time, producing one's best works. However, I could not get out of myself or forget myself because of fatigue and aches. Therefore, I took painkillers and remedies sometimes to improve my feelings, but it did not produce the results I desired, I feel, because one's creative spirit can be restricted when not feeling well.

My system could not function as well as it used to, so I had to face this quandary. My paintings were still mediocre, but I knew I could paint better pictures if only I was well…how annoying. Therefore, acceptance and taking a day at a time was all I could possibly do. Sometimes when I felt a bit better, an on-and-off thing, I would undertake more activities, do some gardening, and try painting.

In addition, the skin on my body was starting to come out in melanomas, which are life threatening skin cancers from past exposure to the sun. I had the first cut out, which was half the size of an apple, and they made such a mess that I decided to search for other ways. I believe the Lord led me to a special black salve, which after application follows the roots of the cancer down to eliminate it all. Several more melanoma cancers developed shortly after in different areas, yet the cream fixed them all by eating out the cancer. It will only attack cancerous cells, not healthy cells. Where it dissolved the cancer, it left holes in me so large one could see the muscles and sinews it had worked past, yet the final healing was miraculous where one could hardly see where it had been. **See Psalm 23:4 (NIV) and Psalm 34:17–20 (NIV).** Praise God.

Norma, Jonathan, and I took a break and went up to Cairns by train, which was a long journey. We did a few sightseeing tours, one being out on a large yacht. After a crash course in scuba diving, I swam around the reefs with other amateurs, an unforgettable experience. It was a completely different world underwater, with beautifully coloured fish, coral, and the occasional large clam.

Chapter 23

Looking to God Again for Healing

*J*started to look to God again for answers, acceptance of my condition, and to try to find peace of mind and more happiness, a spiritual journey I guess. *In the Bible, Paul was gifted with spiritual power to help others, yet God required him to remain humbled and disabled to a degree so that it would be seen that it was God who gave Paul a special anointing to work for Him, and not his own power. So perhaps like Paul, God must have an important task for me, and that surely must be to testify about Him through my own experiences.* See in part **Isaiah 49:7 (NIV):** *"because of the Lord, who is faithful, the Holy One of Israel, who has chosen you."*

God had to tell Paul that His grace was sufficient for him when Paul asked to be healed, and there was a lesson to learn. Paul realised eventually that with his weakness, he was strong through reliance upon God's help so that he could not brag of his own achievements. He says in **2 Corinthians 12:9–10 (NIV)**, *"But he said to me, "My grace is sufficient for you, for my power is made perfect in weakness." Therefore, I will boast all the more gladly about my weaknesses, so Christ's power may rest on me. That's why, for Christ's sake I delight in weaknesses, in insults in hardships, in persecutions, in difficulties. For when I am weak, then I am strong."* As I type this and form in my mind what I am telling you here, I am getting a wonderful spiritual touch, or tingling, in my head. I realise God is telling me so; this is what He wants me to tell you.

He did not remain this way because of any sin or lack of faith; God used this as an example that we should always give Him the glory rather than ourselves. This is one important reason why healing does not always occur. This is a lesson in humility and the need to look to God for our strength, to give God the glory, and not give up if not healed. We should not think it might be due to sin or lack of faith yet realize that God may still have the glory sitting on our shoulders for a special purpose, just as He had done for Paul and has done for so many other people with some thorn in their flesh or disability. Some of these people have aspired to far greater heights than those with all their colours flying. People like this are a great inspiration to others, such as those in the para-olympics or those who paint beautiful pictures by working their brushes with their mouth. *For many of them, this is done through looking to a higher power or God for their skill.*

I knew prayer could be effective for healing, but my faith was rusty. I remembered that it was important not to confess my illness and that my healing was achieved through the cross, but commanding the evil one to depart in Jesus' name had all but slipped considerably from my mind. I believe that God gives us other options, including doctors, natural healing, remedies, and many other methods, all meant to help people cope if a miracle does not occur. I believe He does not have the attitude of *have enough faith or too bad*, for that is not love, and He knows many people cannot muster enough faith. Some miracles may require very strong faith of the ailing person or from others prayers, and yet healing is still up to the Lord's discretion. For although He desires our healing, He has a bigger picture than we do as sometimes there are very good reasons for delays in healing. This particularly applies when it will help many people.

However, I can only touch on a little of what the Bible has to offer as it can provide answers to many of life's questions, and the information it gives will inspire a person to go on seeking. See **James 1:2 (NIV)**: *"Consider it pure joy, my brothers and sisters, whenever you face trials of many kinds, because you know that the testing of your faith produces perseverance. Let perseverance finish its work so that you maybe mature and complete, not lacking anything."* Also see **Romans 5:3–5 (NIV)**: *"Not only so, but we also glory in our sufferings, because we know that suffering produces perseverance; perseverance, character; and character, hope. And hope does not put us to shame, because God's love has been poured out into our hearts through the Holy*

Spirit, who has been given to us." So if we can see difficulties and disappointments in life as a challenge, and even a blessing in disguise, and not be defeated by them, we will grow in character; by holding onto the Lord with faith, He will honor our perseverance. It will be worthwhile for us. See also **Jeremiah 20:11 (NIV):** *"But the Lord is with me like a mighty warrior so my persecutors will stumble and not prevail. They will fail and be thoroughly disgraced; their dishonor will never be forgotten."*

My faith was not strong enough at that time for total healing as before, when praying over others. Yet then again, maybe God wanted me to be like Paul and continue to realise that it is better to rely on Him and grow spiritually so that I would eventually write this book, thus helping many more to grow in faith. So I prayed then for guidance to find the right natural remedies and medicines to help alleviate symptoms, and sure enough, the Lord led me to some that helped. I read recently in **Isaiah 40:30–31 (NIV)** *"Even youths grow tired and weary, and young men stumble and fall; but those who hope in the Lord will renew their strength. They will soar on wings like eagles; they will run and not grow weary, they will walk and not be faint."* God saved my life many times and used my illness to be a blessing so that I would also eventually help others. It is better to be physically weakened and have a relationship with God than to be physically well without Him.

For example, if I had a need, such as when I had lost something, after praying, I would find it; praying especially for a parking space was successful also. If I forgot to pray, my search was unsuccessful. Sometimes a tingling feeling in the head would be present when praying alone, or with church groups, or when thinking positive Christian thoughts or ideas, which God would agree with. Therefore, knowing God is there with one and guiding a person can be comforting, especially if they have been through difficult times. Life can still be difficult, but sometimes difficulties bring blessings. With regard to money, this is not just having much money, where people might still be miserable, but rather an attitude of prosperity even if one is battling financially. If a person claims prosperity with true faith, they can receive it and gain peace of mind. This principle applies to other needs as well. See **Mark 11:23–24 (NIV) and Matthew 21:22 (NIV)**. *"If you believe, you will receive whatever you ask for in prayer."* Needs may take time to achieve, such as healing, as God knows what's best for humanity and has His perfect timing, so patience may be necessary, but I found that knowing God and having a believing faith made a difference. However, our desires should not be the reason to look to God, as we should look to Him firstly with praise, thankfulness, and love because of His love and what He has done for us through His son Jesus. See **Matthew 6:33 (NIV)**. *"But seek first His kingdom and His righteousness and all these things will be given to you as well."*

However, healing may not occur because God has a higher purpose in mind so that many people are helped as seen in the following example. *There was a minister who despite having a heart attack, knew the importance of praising God even for this, like his family also had learnt to do, rather than complaining, because they knew God had a reason; consequently, God didn't immediately heal him. In hospital, he managed to testify about the wonderful works of God and Christ Jesus, to a patient next to him. This patient was so impressed that he went out into the world, became an evangelist, and preached the Gospel, consequently bringing many thousands of people to accept and know Jesus as their saviour. This would not have happened if this minister did not have the heart attack. Here you can see a wonderful example of God's reasoning and knowing what is best.*

Perhaps also it has been the evil one trying to get me in my close escapes so I could not testify to the eminence of our God. Yet God saved me from his grasp many times so that I would eventually accept Jesus as my saviour. Read **Ephesians 2:4–9 (NIV):** *"But because of His great love for us, God who is rich in mercy, made us alive with Christ even when were dead in transgressions—it is by grace you have been saved And God raised us up with Christ and seated us with him in the heavenly realms in Christ Jesus, so in the coming ages he might show the incomparable riches of his grace, expressed in his kindness to us in Christ Jesus. For it is by grace you have been saved, through faith—and this not from yourselves, it is the gift of God—not by works, so no one can boast."*

I personally tried to cover up my symptoms with remedies so that I could socialise better; however, these also had side effects. Researchers actually discovered that an infection or toxins plus stress cause CFS, usually causing a malfunction of the mitochondria (the energy mechanisms), which are the powerhouses within cell nuclei producing energy.

I found, though, it is best to try to focus on the present positively and look forward to a better future, knowing the freedom given through what Jesus had done with a joyful and renewed attitude. Read **Isaiah 43:18 (NIV):** *"Forget the former things; do not dwell on the past."* And in **Philippians 3:13–14 NIV,** in part, *"But one thing I do: Forgetting what is behind and straining toward what is ahead, I press on toward the goal to which the prize for which God has called me heavenward in Jesus Christ."*

Although some traumas in my life had also affected me in some ways, it brought me to rely on God and to have faith, and this is far more important. Learning how to know and tune into God is so important, especially when stressed, in order to retain balance. Nowadays there is too much going on, too much noise, and people are racing here, there, and everywhere, trying to find peace and joy through so many activities, when the only true peace and joy are found with God and Christ Jesus. It is very important to stop and "smell the roses", as the saying goes, or meditate on peaceful nature, peaceful music, or something tranquil that God has created. He gave us all these things for our benefit, good health, and balance.

I found it beneficial on a daily basis to drop all thoughts or worries and "STOP"; take a deep breath and relax, let go, stay in the moment, and visualize Jesus, or a favorite peaceful scene. Then by praying a prayer of praise and thankfulness to the Lord, I would ask Him to give me peace and show Himself to me, often speaking in tongues from the Holy Spirit as the disciples did, and like many others do who I know, testifying to its amazing power, which is our perfect communication language with God, expressing exactly what is needed for a better life, and somehow invoking a much deeper feeling of peace and joy, than our normal prayers achieve, believe me it really makes such a difference, see **Acts 2:4 (NIV)** *all of them were filled with the Holy spirit and began to speak in other tongues as the Spirit enabled them.* Then I would "WAIT" for the touch of the Holy Spirit sending His healing light through my body, and sure enough, I would start to get a tingling in my head, sometimes waves of it flowing down through my body, with a wonderful feeling of relaxation, peace, and joy. Instead of resuming work, I would "STAY" in His presence for as long as possible, for then a wonderful relationship and understanding with God can grow. This was a blessing, and is a well-known tried and tested method of finding more peace, and tuning into God, so it also helped my faith.

I needed these times to help recover, rebalance, and heal. See **Matthew 11:28–30 (NIV):** *"Come to me all you weary and burdened and I will give you rest. Take my yoke upon you and learn from me for I am gentle and humble in heart, and you will find rest for your souls. For my yoke is easy and my burden is light."* In addition, see **John 14:27 (NIV):** *"Peace I leave with you; my peace I give you. I do not give to you as the World gives. Do not let your hearts be troubled and do not be afraid."* Also, read **Philippians 4:7 (NIV).** *"And the peace of God, which transcends all understanding, will guard your hearts and your minds in Christ Jesus."*

I found that God started to hear my prayers more when I attempted to forgive others. In the Bible, I found Jesus preached this; see **Luke 6:37–38 (NIV):** *"Do not judge, and you will not be judged. Do not condemn, and you will not be condemned. Forgive, and you will be forgiven. Give, and it will be given to you."* Forgiveness all-round was so important for God to hear my prayers—and for us all. Giving and helping others are also of importance for blessings, fulfilment, peace, and happiness to come one's way. Jesus' sacrifice for us was amazing, having been predicted in the Old Testament long before He was born; see **Isaiah 53:4–6 (NIV)** and **Matthew 27:47–50 (NIV)** in the New Testament.

Having accepted Jesus as my saviour and being baptised and filled with the Holy Spirit was apparently so important for me to work effectively as a Christian and to help decipher the true meaning of what the word said, not just gaining head knowledge of the Bible, but putting it permanently into my heart. Ongoing reading of the word plus related reading, fellowship with a church group, and going to church became inspirational, helping me grow in the Lord and in faith.

Difficulties have become a revelation to me in being able to use them to help others as the Lord said to Paul in 2 Corinthians 12:9. Therefore, instead of complaining about things in life, I could praise God in all difficulties, knowing that God had a purpose, finding that the Lord could turn difficulties into blessings, and being able to stand on and rely on His word and promises. They may not immediately eventuate, but His word has stood the test of time with countless others. Focusing on helping others and showing compassion or help was fulfilling and a blessing. See Philippians 2:4.

Laughing with others, keeping a sense of humour, being positive and believing in, and knowing oneself as God sees us is therapeutic—God has a high opinion of us. As Job said after all his suffering and loss in **Job 23:10 (NIV)**, *"but he knows the way that*

I take: when he has tested me, I will come forth as gold". Through Job's faith in the Lord, like David, God blessed him in the end.

In the Bible, it also says in **Romans 8:28 (NIV)**, *"and we know that in all things God works for the good of those who love him, who have been called according to his purpose"*. Another helpful one was **1 John 4:4 (NIV)**: *"You dear children, are from God and have overcome them, because the one who is in you, is greater than the one who is in the world."* In other words, God is stronger than the evil one in the world.

In addition, when troubles and problems beset me, I looked to the verse I mentioned before in **John 14:27 (NIV)**, where Jesus says, *"Peace I leave with you; my peace I give you. I do not give to you as the world gives. Do not let your hearts be troubled and do not be afraid."*

I realised God can create blessings, triumphs, and victories out of suffering. He could turn my life around. I might still have some difficulties, but I would see them in a new light, and my burden thus would lighten. The light would shine through the darkness for me. Through all my difficulties, I found these particular verses provided much relief and clarity of purpose to me, knowing they are the Lord's promises and have helped many people like me in the hardest times of their life to carry on with hope and not give up. In addition, by giving, one shall receive, and a generous heart prospers much; see **Proverbs 11:25 (NIV)**: *"A generous person will prosper; whoever refreshes others will be refreshed."* By helping and praying for others, you are helping yourself also in the healing process.

Chapter 24

Life on the Island

We joined a church on the island and became involved in church life and community organisations. Norma taught Sunday school and was Secretary and Treasurer of the church as well as the boat club. Our children went to school on the island. It was a delightful place to swim at the front of our house, catch fish from our small beach, or mud crabs from pots placed in the mangroves. I had a small pond built by a friend at the bottom of the cliff, used like a spa for cooling under a small waterfall in summer, and it was refreshing to relax in on a hot night while listening to the waves roll in nearby. Soaking in cool water helps CFS sufferers, and I found this and the peaceful views very therapeutic.

We had a stone fireplace for bar-b-cues to sit around and chat with friends at night-time. This area under shady trees was a special place for us, especially when some species of birds would visit — it felt spiritual. We also had another delightful sandy beach with clear water to swim in that was only a forty-second walk from our boundary. Nearby were oyster-covered rocks and delightful coral reefs, which I would dive over occasionally, seeing many coloured fish. Farther out, we would occasionally see dolphins surfacing, looking for fish. I had a rowing boat and a larger fifteen-foot half cabin with an outboard motor, brought from Melbourne by truck.

When I was able and feeling a bit better, we took the boat out and did some fishing, and Glen, Jonathan, and I explored the islands from Macleay to Southport near Surfers Paradise and as far north as Tangalooma on Moreton Island. We had some wonderful trips, especially when our families, friends, and relatives visited us.

The boat motor at one stage broke down, so we had to call for help on the radio to have the boat towed. After two such incidents, I decided to purchase a more reliable reconditioned motor. Other times I had to brave dangerous and difficult conditions to get home, as Moreton Bay had a nasty habit of blowing up suddenly; as the bay was shallow, treacherous wave conditions would develop.

After joining a fishing club, a fishing expedition to the exposed ocean side of Moreton Island on a fishing trawler, found us in rough conditions off the Island. I was in the captain's pilot cabin having a chat with him, and suddenly a gigantic whale surfaced right under the bow of the boat. As he had not seen it, I said, "Look out, there's a whale under the boat", so he quickly steered it sideways off the whale to avoid a collision. He turned the boat to follow the whale, but a large pod of dolphins came beside the trawler, blocking us and trying to veer us away from the whale. I thought, "How marvellous these intelligent mammals are, trying to protect some fellow mammals." Dolphins throughout history have saved the lives of many human beings also. Wild dolphins have carried shipwrecked human beings ashore on their backs and surrounded humans to protect them from sharks. God is wonderful in His creations, having given them all a purpose.

The whales travel yearly to the Antarctic to feed, then travel back to nurse their young, and rest farther north around Fraser Island, providing a wonderful tourist attraction there. We spent some pleasant holiday time with a very thoughtful couple, Tom and Cris, on Fraser Island, including whale watching there. It was spectacular. Another fishing trip with Tom—Norma's sister Cris's husband—and Jonathan on a charter fishing boat to the eastern side of Moreton Island saw us catching many snapper, a large Cobia by one chap, and a large 13kg Jew fish by myself. These were good fishing waters at times, but care was necessary when crossing the shallow, turbulent sandbar areas between North Stradbroke and Morton Island.

We also spent many great times with Alan and Judith (Norma's cousin) and their boys Ronny and Lionel, showing them around when they visited from South Australia. Many of our families and cousins from Australia and New Zealand came to stay with us, and we had enjoyable times, including taking them around in the boat.

I had many interesting discussions while on the island, particularly with a friend Richard, originally from Melbourne who had a very responsible position working for Myers. He was also an artist, with a great sense of humour, interested in plants, and very well read, being knowledgeable on many subjects, including world history. Another friend, David, also very bright, was quite interesting to talk to, especially about Christian and spiritual matters. Learning of his beliefs and spiritual experiences, helped increase my faith.

I went to New Zealand again for Aunty June's 80th birthday and saw many cousins, including new additions, and hired a car to travel through the Haast Pass again, then to Queenstown and back to Christchurch. I wanted to fly into Milford Sound, but the weather made flying too dangerous. I felt the cold much more this time, especially in Queenstown.

One sunny Saturday, our church group was having a picnic on another island nearby, called Coochiemudlo Island, where Matthew Flinders had landed while exploring Moreton Bay, thinking it was a river system. They asked me to bring all the food across in my boat, while the rest of the church members went ahead on a ferry to the island. Well, the car motor would not start; later I found that a rat had eaten through electrical wires under the dashboard. I needed the car to tow and launch the boat. Anyway, it was a calm day and only about one-and-a-half kilometres across to Coochiemudlo, so I thought I would take the small boat having a two horsepower outboard motor on it, as I had to get the food to them somehow.

I got across easily, and after having a pleasant day, Norma and Jonathan wanted to come back in the small boat with me. The water still looked calm on our side of the island, but as we left the protection of the island, it got choppy. As we approached the channel, the little motor stopped, causing the

boat to go sideways and then swamped by a wave. The boat was full of water, only held up by air locks at the bow and under the seats, so the top of the boat was only about two centimetres above sea level. We were in a hazardous situation, the waves were getting larger, and if we fell out of the boat, the strong current would sweep us away. Norma could not swim well, and Jonathan was only small, with some dog paddling experience.

Norma was crying and praying at the same time, so I went into emergency mode and put life jackets on them quickly. I told them if they were washed out, to hold onto the boat, each other, or me, and not panic. I then gave Norma a bucket and told her to bail the water; however, Jonathan was in the wrong position, so we had to get him to crouch between the seats in the water. We could not risk moving too much, and I had to start rowing the boat back a long way to the Coochiemudlo shores. Going towards Macleay would be too treacherous.

We finally arrived back at Coochiemudlo wet, tired, and shocked but alive, thank God. See **Psalm 18:6 (NIV):** *"In my distress I called to the Lord; I cried to my Lord for help. From his temple he heard my voice; my cry came before him, into his ears."* Also, read **Isaiah 43:2 (NIV):** *"When you pass through the waters, I will be with you; and when you pass through the rivers, they will not sweep over you. When you walk through the fire, you will not be burned; the flames will not set you ablaze."* It was wonderful that God was with us; I think I would rather have God than doing it alone—too risky, I reckon.

Again, our prayers were answered. God surely heard Norma's prayer. It is a miracle none of us were lost. I thanked God sincerely as this would have been terrible. I decided I would have to leave the boat on Coochiemudlo for a while because of the conditions, so I prayed for help to carry it to somebody's house. Suddenly, a large Polynesian chap with powerful arms like a rugby player came strolling along, so I asked him if he would not mind helping. He picked the boat up on his own and held it above his head. I had not tried carrying it this way myself before…*"hmm"*. *Wow, another prayer answered!*

This is another example of where God puts people in the right place at the right time to help others. He carried it all the way over his head to a house, where they gladly held the boat for me until I came and towed it back with my larger boat. I suppose one could think the evil one was trying to get us by making that rat chew through the wires under the dashboard. In all the years I have had a car, this was the only time it happened; it makes one wonder. However, the Lord again turned a very dangerous situation around by showing His power to overcome.

Some church members came to our house to check if we had come home safely, as they were very worried. They prayed together for our safety as they could not see our boat or see us across the bay that afternoon. Read **Psalm 46:1–2 (NIV).** *"God is our refuge and strength, an ever-present help in trouble. Therefore we will not fear, though the Earth give way and the mountains fall into the heart of the sea."*

Life on the Island

Richard, Donna's husband, and I came back from Peel Island against sudden hazardous conditions one day, where strong winds and rough waters prevailed; however, the boat handled the waves admirably. They advised over the radio to stay at Peel Island, but Richard had to get back. This was not the only time it happened to me, but these types of conditions had troubled many boaties in Moreton Bay.

I also had a scooter for a while, to save on fuel costs, and one day the front wheel jammed in thick sand in a road gutter when I was entering another street. I fell off the scooter, and it landed on top of me, the hot exhaust pipe burning my legs and crushing my foot. Somebody helped me to my feet, but I could not walk, and had to go around on crutches for some time.

One night the blinding lights of a car caused me to go into the gravel off the bitumen, and the bike swerved sideways; however, I just managed to control it, fortunately, as I was travelling at about 52 kilometres per hour, which could have been serious had I come off. The small wheels of a scooter are less stable in loose gravel than those of a motorbike.

Another time, when having to trim some tree branches, a branch broke under my feet, and I fell probably eight feet to the ground. My head just missed a log by one or two centimetres. It could have finished me if my head had hit the log, as the impact of my face on the ground made it split open like a watermelon, so I had to get many stitches to my face; see **Psalm 23:4 (NIV)** and **Psalm 34:19–20 (NIV)**. *"A righteous man may have many* *troubles, but the Lord delivers him from them all; he protects all his bones, not one will be broken."*

Sometimes I had to stay alone on the island, and one day I walked on the coral reef; however, I was taking an antibiotic for an infection at the time. When I went to bed, my tongue jammed up and I could not breathe; nobody was there to help me. I instantly grabbed an antihistamine tablet, which saved my life I believe, as the anaphylactic shock slowly subsided. These are very dangerous. **Psalm 23:4 (NIV)** and **Psalm 34:17–20 (NIV)**. This can happen to anybody allergic to anything. I should have rung the ambulance immediately as I was told to get an adrenaline injection, but as I recovered, I did not bother. Now I am not sure if it was something I stepped on, on the reef or the antibiotic that caused it.

I was lying under a shady tree one day next to the small pool built into the cliff, and a snake came through the ferns and crossed straight over my stomach; I was in its path, so again, I am not sure who got the biggest surprise. I had carried a large carpet snake out of our garage by the tail before, but this was a big surprise. It was not a very pleasant feeling.

Another time I was fishing off one of the mangrove trees, using berley with tuna oil in it. As the day was getting hot, I decided to prop the rod in a branch and have a quick swim to cool down. As I was swimming, I noticed a large, long black shape swimming next to me. Realising it was a shark, around four feet long, I scrambled back up the mangrove tree. I was not sure what type of shark it was, however Bull sharks were known to be in the northern parts of the bay, and had taken a woman swimming on North Stradbroke

Island; they were living in the canals along the Gold Coast and nearby Raby Bay. Swimming in the canals is unwise; however, the likelihood of attack is very rare in the bay.

Norma also helped in the local primary school to support children in their reading and writing program, in the tuckshop, and being a uniform convenor for the school. I was doing paintings and putting them in exhibitions and art galleries around Brisbane. Having the privilege of exhibiting required us to take turns in voluntary running of the galleries for one day a month. This included making sales, care of monies, writing records, counting petty cash, and many other duties involved in running a shop or gallery. This was an interesting experience I had in two galleries, one of which I exhibited alongside some famous artists. It was indeed a privilege to be doing this. However, just getting there was a trial when not feeling the best from the CFS, and I sometimes had to cancel my duty. I also helped run the island gallery at some stages and did some art teaching on the island for a short time.

I wanted to get on with life as much as I could and not miss opportunities, so I performed duties often through sheer willpower despite my body not cooperating properly at times, and I would often cover up my pain with painkillers and remedies.

One evening I took the family from Macleay in the boat to Raby Bay Harbour, moored there, and went to a Christmas carol-singing event, afterwards returning to Macleay at night. The evening was ideal and the sea calm, with many lights reflecting on the water. We passed a small ship on the way back, and travelling in the boat at night on a calm sea is like flying in a light aircraft; the water is so black that it is rather like being airborne.

I came home to the island from the mainland where I usually spent a week or so at Bettina's flat, after having an uncanny feeling that something was wrong at home, and upon arriving I could smell smoke in the house. Apparently, one of the neighbours I later found out had tried to burn off some rubbish down near the bay and eventually put it out. However, during the afternoon, a hot wind came up and the fire started up again rather viciously. I yelled to him to put it out while I called the fire brigade; however, it quickly got out of hand, and his garden hose was useless. It started roaring up the hill towards our house, the trunks of trees bursting into flame, and knowing there were plenty of dry gum leaves in our gutters, I was up onto our roof with a hose, aided by a ladder and another neighbour within a very short time; it is amazing what a little adrenaline can do. Flying ashes on fire were actually setting fire to the flammable leaves in the gutters, and the bushes right next to our home were on fire; however, I just managed to put them out as the fire brigade people started to get the fire under control. It was a miracle getting home just in time to save our home from this fire. As gum trees surrounded our home, it does not take long for the gutters to fill with dry leaves, so even regular clean-ups still were not enough. It is a fact that gum leaves in gutters are a big fire risk to homes. Again, I thank God for making me come home. Praise God.

Psalm 25:15 (NIV): *"My eyes are ever on the Lord, for only He will release my feet from the snare."*

See Isaiah 43:2 (NIV). *"When you pass through the waters, I will be with you; and when you pass through the rivers, they will not sweep over you. When you walk through the fire, you will not be burned; the flames will not set you ablaze."*

In 2008, we went to New Zealand for a family reunion. This was a wonderful time. On arrival, we went to a Maori concert, which included a presentation of their culture and way of life in the past. Although, sadly, Dad, Uncle Philip, and Ken could not be there, we saw their children and grandchildren, our cousins, including Ruth and Ron, Sue and Steven, Anne, Carol, Philippa and Colin, their children, and Aunty Leah, all wonderful cousins. Many whom we had not met before were from all parts of New Zealand.

The reunion was held at our Aunt's house, called "Riverside"; there were many speeches, and I recited a poem I had written about our experiences at Riverside as children. John, Wilma, Andrea, Jacqueline, Karen, Matthew, and their families from Australia were also there. I am grateful that Nick and Annette, Trish and Tim, Geoff and Sue, and many others organized it so well, especially Nick and Catherine for studying our ancestry. Forgive me if I have forgotten to mention anybody. In addition, it was wonderful seeing Aunty June again. There were around one hundred and fifty people there.

We spent the first evening at the home of Nick and Annette followed the next day with the reunion at Riverside. Then there was a party at the Amberley domain hall, which was decorated with many photographs of our ancestors, including one of our family trees. There were many very interesting speeches, and bagpipes played celebrating our part-Scottish heritage from my Grandmother Catherine Smith's ancestry. The following day we attended a church service and made a visit to the cemetery, where many of our ancestors lay, followed by another get-together at Tim and Trish's home.

After the reunion, we travelled in a motor home to Hamner Springs, where a good soak in the healing mineral waters was welcome. The small pools were designed and built with a natural appearance, each having a different temperature, thus making the whole experience more interesting. Our long journey the next day took us to see our old home at Mariri, followed by a stay overnight near Motueka. Jonathan and I took turns in driving, as some journeys were long.

We travelled through picturesque countryside along the Haast Pass and spent the next night near the Franz Josef Glacier, which we climbed along on the next day. It was a remarkable experience walking on the ice glacier with its deep blue chasms, which could be treacherous if one was not careful. We had to wear special clothing and proper ice boots called crampons and use walking axes. It looked, seemed, and felt as though it was the Antarctic it was so cold. It was exhausting for me, and I limped wearily on the way back; fortunately, I had taken some CoQ10 tablets for energy, the best remedy of only a few I eventually discovered that temporarily helped my fatigue problems.

We travelled on to Queenstown, where we flew in a small plane across the snow-capped mountains to Milford Sound. The journey was spectacular as we flew close to the snow-covered peaks and then descended through a valley to the Sounds. Milford Sound is an old valley running down to the sea, cut out by a glacier long ago; a boat journey on the sounds held us in awe of its magnificence. The deep blue-green water was surrounded by towering cliffs and peaks on either side, reaching up seemingly forever; piercing the clouds, where the occasional waterfall magically appeared dropping back through the clouds to end its descent in a misty collision with the glassy water below. It was like a dream world, mystical, so delightful, and rewarding to the senses.

The next day saw us trying an exhilarating jet-boat ride, which weaved its way treacherously at high speed through a narrow river gorge, just missing rocky outcrops on the sides, followed by full circle spins of the boat that threw us heavily against the sides, a bit of an adrenaline booster. Luckily, we had confidence in the driver. We also went on a steam train ride, which brought back old memories. Then, finally, we headed back towards Christchurch after going up on a gondola to look over the Remarkables (snow-covered mountains) and picturesque Lake Wakatipu, with Queenstown nestled at the bottom.

We visited majestic Mount Cook, which fascinated my family, then a salmon and trout farm where colossal fish chased the food pellets thrown to them. We stayed the night at Lake Tekapo surrounded by panoramic snow-capped mountains. There was a quaint, yet famous little church called "The Church of the Good Shepherd" built out on a protruding arm of Lake Tekapo's shore. I wondered how many congregations would have been mesmerised by the beautiful views, thus praising God, as the minister preached in the early days. Its views included copy perfect reflections of snow-capped mountains on the serene lake.

We settled in back at Christchurch and visited Philippa and Colin for the evening, having a nice time with them. Sadly, recently we heard that Colin passed away in a farm accident, a big shock for Philippa and her family, and all of us, especially as he was a great chap.

The next day we explored Lyttelton Harbour then Christchurch with its charming old buildings, the museum, Christchurch Cathedral Church, spectacular flower beds, with the Avon River meandering through the gardens, just as we had seen them when children. Sadly, soon after this visit, as I mentioned, the earthquakes caused much destruction here. Mount Cook, on the front cover of this book is symbolic of spiritual aspirations many of us have, not only showing one of God's beautiful creations, but it also reminds me of the wonderfully uplifting words in Jesus greatest speech, "Sermon on the Mount", called the "Beatitudes", see Matthew 5:1-12.

When I was doing a painting of Mount Cook in a different light, I was playing inspiring, creative music at the time as I found that it helped me produce far better paintings. When I look into some areas of my paintings where my spirit kicks in, I am amazed and say to myself, "I didn't do that, did I?" I could see in the hills at the foot of Mount Cook where my spirit painted; I cannot remember creating all the detail shown. Great, I had discovered the secret to painting better pictures again, using creative music when feeling better, what a relief, praise God, the Holy Spirit took over to produce a better painting. My spirit virtually danced my brush around, and I looked at it later with amazement; my spirit was dancing with joy with the music, and so was the brush.

Although our time on Macleay Island was difficult financially, I felt it was still a blessing in many ways, but the time came when Norma wanted to sell up, and I was feeling like a change as well, as we started to feel the island was limiting our lives. Although I was in a boat club, and visited friends, and went to a small church there, we desired to experience more of what the mainland had to offer.

We stayed on the property for as long as possible, hoping for an increase in its value, but eventually decided to sell. We advertised with some real estate agents, and it took another year or so, until we had a buyer from the island. Over that period, we had to maintain the house and property in good condition to help sell it, and I made a few improvements here and there. In addition, it was a bit annoying during the year having to keep the house and garden extra clean for people to see; however, I had to make the most of it.

Chapter 25

Life on the Mainland

We had been praying and believing God would answer our prayers for a home on the mainland that suited our needs. Norma saw our future home on the Internet shortly after finding a buyer for our home on the island. She said it just stood out and caught her attention immediately. Just newly on display, we looked at it and said, "Yes, it's the one", and the price was suitable. Fortunately, we were the first to see the property, as several others wanted it also—how wonderful God is.

Finally, through searching real estate online, we found and bought this nice home, and fortunately, the property had a shed for gear, somewhere I thought one day that I might have a painting studio. We knew that by claiming anything desired with faith, it would eventuate. See **Mark 11:23–24 (NIV),** where Jesus says, *"I tell you the truth, if anyone says to this mountain, "Go throw yourself into the sea, and does not doubt in his heart, but believes* *what he says will happen, it will be done for him. Therefore, I tell you, whatever you ask for in prayer, believe you have received it, and it will be yours."*

It took a year of patience to sell our property, but the Lord answered our prayers for the needs we had prayed for—a home in an area suitable for Norma to travel to work. I had prayed for a shed and trees, which eventuated, and the trees created a wonderful sound when the wind blew, and were wonderful to gaze upon. The Lord had His perfect timing to find exactly what we needed just at the time of selling our house. Prior to this, we had not seen any suitable home for the price we desired for over a year of searching online.

We had a small pool and rock wall with a waterfall put in, adding the final touches from my past landscaping experience. This gave a small, natural, relaxing scene emulating nature to look at from our patio.

There is joy in the serenity and beauty of nature and the sound of good music that I believe God gives us for joy and relaxing times. We were fortunate to have bushland nearby, where we could walk to a picturesque reservoir, which when viewed, astonishingly resembled the view to Coochiemudlo Island we had from our veranda on the island.

I managed to get away into the country camping and exploring areas north of Brisbane, climbing the hills, and getting photographs for future paintings, especially river scenes. I set up camp along the upper reaches of the Brisbane River. Waking in the morning to the sunrise over the hills and the sight of steam rising off the river, which created enchanting sounds as it flowed over a rocky bottom, with birds cheerfully welcoming the sunrise, was uplifting.

I wandered up alongside the river and into a valley to see if I could spot any wildlife. Sitting down on a rock to rest and gazing along the winding river, its serene water adorned with reflections, a few ducks enjoying their morning paddle. On either side, the green river flats with a few grazing cattle gave way to gum-covered hillsides, that stretched back to merge into the distant blue hills. I listened to the sounds of the bush and looked down to see the tiny ants following each other, busy with their daily chores, and stopping to say hello or passing a message on to their fellow ants going in the opposite direction. Birds were talking and singing to each other far away, and a gentle breeze caressed my face. I felt this was God saying, *"Hello, John, I am here with you and always will be. Do you like the beauty I have created for you and all mankind?"*

I found those moments in my life were very special. It is wonderful to know God is there for company and as a companion, especially when one can feel peace and serenity when surrounded by God's wonderful creations. Tuning into Him was a joy.

I found if I looked to Him, then He was there as company if I tried to seek Him through prayer especially. There is a feeling somehow that you are not alone, so I found Him more so when at peace within myself. Occasionally, in those special quiet moments, especially when in the countryside, I felt He was trying to say, *"Hello, I want to chat to you. Look at all the beauty I have created for you; the sun and moonshine at night for you to see your way and the magnificent wondrous universe and stars above, in all their array, for you to gaze at and be amazed at; the mountains, valleys, and shimmering waters, the animals, birds, plants, flowers, music, and every living thing. The beauty I put here is to make people happy because I love you all. You can talk with me. I want to help you; don't try to do it on your own."* God speaks to us like this in the Bible.

Visiting and staying overnight at the Crystal Waters Permaculture village was fun. The village, designed for sustainable living, has many people residing there. It is a picturesque spot in a valley near a fast flowing stream. It holds special days for many types of events, such as "wellness days" and "back to Earth living" days. I came home feeling as though I had been more in touch with God again and more rejuvenated, especially after spending time chatting to people there, making new friends, and sitting around the campfire with guitars and interesting folks.

I found it was important for me to get back to nature more often—even just going to Tambourine Mountain—as it somehow rejuvenated my mind, body, and spirit. Being in the hills provided fresh air, more oxygen, and more serenity than the hustle-and-bustle environment of the cities, although I found some social life in the city and suburbs was helpful for a balanced life.

Norma also found it easier and more convenient to work; however, our finances were tight as we had a loan we took out to make improvements to our home and to give the roof an overhaul as well as the need for a better car. We also needed more furniture, a refrigerator, oven replacements, and so forth, so it was not long until the loan mounted up, one we regretted taking.

We enjoyed seeing our Melbourne families, who visited us from time to time, including Diana and Neville and their children Kelly, and Sam, Catherine and her husband Terry, a talented chap, who had been a Headmaster, teacher, and tour guide. And I am very grateful for his kind understanding spirit towards me once when I was in sorrow and his care for my father when he was old. Also Terry and Catherine's clever daughter Donna, a remarkable mother and Member of Parliament, and her good husband Richard and their smart boys Chris, Terrence, Douglas, and Jefferson, and Terry and Catherine's very kind daughter Narelle and her son Matthew. Narelle is also very talented and has a strong belief that today's children should be getting back to nature, and she puts her beliefs into action, which is wonderful, because that is where children become involved and inspired by God's creations. Research has shown that children exposed to nature do better in all aspects of life later on than those living an artificial life relying on technology for their happiness.

Betty and Alan, Bettina's nice grandparents, also came to visit us. Alan was also lucky to be alive, now ninety-three years of age, and I am sure God saved him also, as he was serving in the Royal Australian Navy on the heavy cruiser HMAS *Canberra* supporting American landings at Guadalcanal in the battle of Savo Island during the Second World War. Two torpedoes and over twenty salvos struck the cruiser, causing 193 casualties. Sadly, the ship was eventually scuttled due to incapacity after providing a great service for Australia, over a long period. These included, amongst others, rescues, captures, and serving as an escort ship for convoys in the Indian Ocean, from Fremantle to Cape Town, Colombo, Singapore, and Ceylon, also serving in the Tasman Ocean.

It was also great spending time with Geoff from New Zealand, Aunty June, Carol, and her family. David, Margaret, Shirley, Stan and Lorraine, and Aunty Leah and some of her family also came to see us. Cris, Norma's sister, and her husband Tom, both very generous people, came to see us a number of times from America, and Norma's kind cousin Judith and husband Alan and their boys, Ronnie and Lionel, all spent memorable times with us. Some visited while we were still on the island and some on the mainland. We spent time with most of our family when we visited Melbourne, including Narelle and her good husband Bede and their clever boys, Tom, Michael, and Matthew. It was great to see them all.

One of Norma's young nephews, named John, was employed on one of the cruise ships based in Brisbane, so he was able to spend much time with us during his breaks. He was excited to return to Australia to work on another ship after his holidays, but just prior to departure from the Philippines, he died in a motorbike accident, so his family and friends in the Philippines, including ourselves were all very sad, as he was such a nice chap.

We also had to make some trips to Melbourne due to the loss of family members: Betty, Bettina's grandmother, and my father, Douglas at the age of 84, who I later had a dream about, on the night of his 100th birthday anniversary, having forgotten about this, he reminded me in the dream, telling me he was 100 years old and I said, "but you look too young for that age", how amazing. While in Melbourne, I went with the family to our relative John Coleman's

Life on the Mainland

80th birthday party held at John and Wilma's old farm, a wonderful gathering of family and friends. John was well known by many, including the Premier of Victoria. He was a good Christian and well respected in Gippsland for his great service in helping dairy farmers in Victoria. Sadly, he passed away not long after our visit.

Norma and I managed to get away on a P&O cruise for a week to the Pacific Islands-Noumea, Lifou in New Caledonia, and Port Vila in Vanuatu. This was a wonderful break for us; we needed it, and Norma made many Filipino friends on the ship, the Pacific Dawn. We did several sightseeing tours, learning of the history and cultures of the islands, trying their food, and watching their tribal dances. A helicopter flight over Port Vila was quite an experience. We were interested to learn that our allies occupied Port Vila during the Second World War, and nearby were the filming areas for the film *South Pacific*, a movie I have always enjoyed so much, with its enchanting scenery and songs, such as "Some Enchanted Evening", "Bali Hai", and "Younger Than Springtime". Life on board was relaxing and fun, whether dining out, dancing on the deck, swimming, watching excellent entertainment, or just gazing out to sea.

We find that going to church is such a blessing and joy, where there is kindness, sincere care, and help for humanity, helping one grow in faith in the Lord, learning the word, and bringing one closer to the Lord. There is also help for one another and fellowship, bringing more fulfilment, creation of friendships, and balance in one's life.

We have connect-group meetings, held every two weeks, where we study the word in the Bible, sing, and have discussions on different subjects. Where two or more are together in prayer, God's work is more powerful.

I was also happy to march on Anzac Day through Brisbane with the New Zealand veteran contingent wearing Dad's medals for him to honour his service, and Bettina marched with Mum's medals to honour her nursing and ambulance driving work in Sydney during the war. We went to a get together after the march with the NZ Contingent (Kiwis) on a riverboat; I made friends with some great chaps, and the Maoris sang many hand clapping songs. It was a wonderful day. I was so pleased I made the effort; people thronged the roads by the thousands as we marched and especially cheered on the Kiwis.

I had a gathering just three days before my sixty-fifth birthday, and the Holy Spirit compelled me to speak to my guests about how God saved me so many times. Fortunately, my good friend Geoff was there listening and seemed astounded about some things I had mentioned, yet with that look of belief and curiosity, and I was so pleased he witnessed my speech, hoping it would help his faith; on the morning of my birthday, he sadly died due to ongoing heart problems. He was only 59 and a good father to his children, Nicole and Neil, and a good husband to Elsie. We had happy times with them all over many years. I was quite sad, as he was a great friend. I was hoping that he had accepted Jesus as his saviour. His family were actually very distraught, and since then, we have been praying for their counselling and helping them cope and recover, which has been fulfilling for us. I have found that the knowledge I had gained in the past has helped others.

Later, I had to have a wisdom tooth out; however, during the process, it left a hole through to my sinuses, which was a problem as water was going from my mouth and coming out of my nose, quite inappropriate, and so I had to have my gums cut and sewn over the hole. However, after leaving the dentist, it burst open with much blood, I returned for resewing only to have to have a second lot of injections, which I found out later on could make one pass out, and I was not warned not to drive, otherwise I would not have. After leaving the second time, although feeling reasonably okay and alert, I passed out when driving around a corner at traffic lights with many other cars. I became conscious again about one hundred metres along the road, which had a significant, bend in it, and I had unconsciously stopped at more traffic lights to turn right into a hardware store. There is no way I could have driven there unconsciously without help, which is what happened. There was nobody in the car besides myself. I was unconscious, and so I can only attribute the guidance to God's help, which was so amazing. Preventing me from running into other cars or having an accident was miraculous—saved again by God. See **Psalm 23:4 (NIV)** and **Psalm 34:17–20 (NIV)**.

Bettina and I managed to go to Mum's brother David's 80th birthday at Forbes recently, which was a great success. He is a great chap. We met up with Catherine, Terry, Donna, and Jefferson. It was fortunate Donna was able to go as she was still recovering from a life threatening illness; we had prayed for her healing. David's party was held in Forbes and was a great night with many of his friends and relatives attending followed by a Sunday bar-b-cue, storytelling, and songs with David's nice family—Lloyd, Craig, Shirley, Heather, and friends. It was great to see everybody helping out as David lost his dear wife Margaret through illness a few years ago.

I also went away into the hills for a couple of days to stay with my friends Peter and Vicki on their farm near Nanango and to advise them about care for their tree plantation for future furniture production. They had put in dams and were producing and selling wooden cutting boards and garlic from their property. Peter was clever at welding bits of old metal together into birds and other objects and had won a number of prizes. I also enjoyed catching up with other friends, Robert and Angging, Mike a fishing mate, and Geoff on his farm from time to time. Recently I was asked to join a men's fellowship, where we meet fortnightly at our leader Colin's home, and the lessons and fellowship are of great benefit.

Chapter 26

Conclusion

As I mentioned before, it is my desire that you will not see this book as a complaining session. I am aware one should be positive, as the subconscious mind can be sensitive to any information, whether positive or negative. *However, I have had to mention these issues in my life so that you will see, through my experiences, that God and Christ Jesus are genuine.* It is interesting to learn how God works in our lives to help us so that we may in turn be able to help others and give God the glory. We cannot see God visually while living our earthly existence—we cannot see the wind either, and yet we feel it. Many cultures throughout human history have worshipped God in one form or another, and many still do. Doing so has helped give them strength to cope, confidence, and purpose, not being an excuse for insecurity.

However, there are still those who disbelieve or do not look to Him, which is such a pity. This is only because of false teachings, not knowing God and blaming Him, lack of spiritual knowledge, or lack of spiritual experience. I could summarize by saying that despite our mistakes and mishaps, we have free will and are subject to chance, where the evil one can try to destroy us. *Yet God is greater and shows His unconditional love by saving us and filling us with the Holy Spirit, which in turn empowers and guides us if we learn to tune in and become sensitive to His guidance, and look to God with faith through having accepted Christ Jesus as our saviour—developing a relationship with God through His word and wisdom in the Bible.*

I believe my story demonstrates this truth, especially in the way God can turn our misfortunes into blessings. I am so pleased that I have come to know and appreciate God for what He has done in my life; bringing more peace, happiness, fulfilment, purpose, improved health, and a different perspective on life, such as, where to place material possessions on the importance scale. *I definitely would not like to risk it without Him anymore after experiencing what life can throw our way.* Unfortunately, many have to learn the hard way before they come to the Lord, like a careless person, who afterwards has to live for the rest of their life with the consequences.

Although I am far from perfect myself, yet God used me to show through my experiences that He was there all along saving me and even proving how incredible His love for us all is through the infilling of the Holy Spirit. Because of His amazing love and

Conclusion

care, I realized that surely we should also reciprocate to Him with favour, love, praise, and thanksgiving. Therefore, I praise God in all my difficulties and challenges because they have brought me closer to God, thus encouraging me to write this book to help all who read it. I hope that you have found my stories interesting and of help. One hopes this important information will encourage and give people hope. It is neither possible nor a coincidence that I could have survived all these incidents without God's divine intervention. I will quote some encouraging verses, which should help provide a greater understanding.

We all have a free will, which is better than being like robots. Read **Genesis 1:26 (NIV)**: *"Then God said, 'Let us make man in our image, in our likeness, and let them rule the fish of the sea and the birds of the air, over all the Earth, and over all the creatures that move along the ground."* However, global warming and pollution are examples of abuse of this gift to us. Also, the Bible states in **Ecclesiastes 9:11 (NIV)**, *"but time and chance happen to them all"*, which means that we are all, over time, subject to the possibility that both good and less fortunate things can happen to us. In **1 John 5:19 (NIV)** it says, *"We know we are children of God, and that the world is under the control of the evil one."* However, God reminded me that there is hope and protection, where He answers our needs. In this following promise, we can ask for His help; see **Matthew 7:7 (NIV)**: *"Ask and it will be given to you; seek and you will find; knock and the door will be opened to you"*. Jesus says to us in **John 15:16-17 (NIV)**, *"You did not choose me, but I chose you and appointed you so that you might* *go and bear fruit—fruit that will last—and so that whatever you ask in my name the father will give you. This is my command: Love each other."*

See this promise for protection in **Psalm 23:4 (NIV)**: *"Even though I walk through the valley of the shadow of death, I will fear no evil, for you are with me; your rod and your staff, they comfort me."* Remember **Isaiah 43:2 (NIV)** and **Psalm 34:17–20 (NIV)** *"The righteous cry, and the LORD hears them; he delivers them from all their troubles. The LORD is close to the broken-hearted and saves those crushed in spirit. The righteous person may have many troubles, but the LORD delivers him from them all; he protects all his bones, not one will be broken."*

I found there are many more promises like these that we can claim and rely on in the Bible. Some prayers are not answered immediately, but God can provide the right answer at the right time; it may not be the time or the answer we expect, but He knows what is best for us. Sometimes God allows delays in answering our prayers, and waiting on the Lord is at times not easy—faith and trust are needed. Read **Hebrews 11:1 (NIV)**: *"Now faith is being sure of what we hope for and certain of what we do not see."*

One lesson of utmost importance I realised, despite taking as much care as possible, was the need for care and wisdom about every decision in life by praying about it and making every decision positive for the best possible outcome. I discovered I could achieve this more efficiently by placing my life in God's hands through prayer to follow, trust, and learn from Him. His word in the Bible, where much help and guidance can be found, teaches us and

Conclusion

gives hope as well as purpose in leading a better life. I found that handing over problems to God was wise, as lack of care or incorrect decisions in important matters surely could affect one for the rest of one's life, which happened to me. See **Proverbs 3:5–7 (NIV)**, where it says, *"Trust in the LORD with all your heart and lean not on your own understanding; in all your ways acknowledge him, and he will make your paths straight. Do not be wise in your own eyes; fear the LORD and shun evil."* I would nowadays try to imagine what Jesus would do if He had a similar decision to make. This was not being weak but only sensible in order to achieve the best that life has to offer. I found that serving God and our fellow man brings the most fulfilment, joy, and peace.

Recently I realized that reading the word in the Bible and going to our fellowship meetings increased my faith again, and their prayers and mine for my ailments have improved my health, so I am happy that God is hearing and answering our prayers, bringing more peace and joy into my heart. I realize that it is so important to keep a close relationship with God, the Church, and fellow believers in a connect group, remembering to pray about everything.

I am deeply grateful to God for touching me so miraculously and saving my life so many times, which kept me going and finally prompted me to witness to His amazing unconditional love. **Psalm 116: 1-9 (NIV)** touches my heart, as it almost summarises my story so well, saying, *"I love the Lord, for He heard my voice; He heard my cry for mercy. Because He turned His ear to me, I will call on Him for as long as I live. The cords of death entangled me, the* *anguish of the grave came over me; I was overcome by distress and sorrow. Then I called on the name of the Lord: "Lord, save me!" The Lord is gracious and righteous; our God is full of compassion. The Lord protects the unwary; when I was brought low, He saved me. Return to your rest, my soul, for the Lord has been good to you. For you, Lord, have delivered me from death, my eyes from tears, my feet from stumbling, that I may walk before the Lord in the land of the living."* Therefore, I pray that through this book, you will perceive the reality of God and Christ Jesus, thus developing a personal relationship with Him, and go into the world and spread the good news about Jesus. I sincerely say that you will be blessed for doing this.

By putting my trust in the Lord, He made me a better person through these difficulties. Challenges fortified me, gave me more wisdom, and gave me better values. See **Romans 8:28 (NIV)**: *"And we know that in all things God works for the good of those who love him, who have been called according to his purpose."*

I found consolation and more peace through these following verses; see **1 Samuel 30:6 (NIV)**, where it says, *"But David found strength in the Lord his God."* I also like **Philippians 4:6–7 (NIV)**: *"Do not be anxious about anything, but in everything, by prayer and petition, with thanksgiving, present your requests to God. And the peace of God, which transcends all understanding, will guard your hearts and your minds in Christ Jesus."* See also two valuable promises in **Philippians 4:13 (NIV)**: *"I can do everything through him who gives me strength."* See also **Philippians**

4:19 (NIV): *"And my God will meet all your needs according to his glorious riches in Christ Jesus."*

People like Job and David in the Bible went through exceptionally difficult times but kept trusting in the Lord; by doing so, I also became blessed in the end. I learnt that those who rely on their own understanding or those without difficulties often do not come to God and thus can miss blessings and end in defeat and destruction. Examples of this are seen in the Old Testament, where generations of people who had it good and rejected God finished up by delivery into slavery, but those with difficulties who yet relied on God became blessed.

I found, like many others, that there are many verses in the Bible like this that show God will help and support us through times of trouble and that He can even turn bad events into blessings if we will just put our trust and faith in Him. What would our lives be like without challenges and difficulties? Could life be boring? Learning from difficulties makes us grow. Perhaps we would be lesser beings without these challenges to improve and strengthen us.

Through difficult experiences, I have discovered that we can learn, gain wisdom, teach, and warn others for their benefit so that they may avoid pitfalls in life. Many criminals and wrongdoers have received a change of heart through finding God, and other people who have been through difficult times will testify to the joy, relief, and blessings of finding and trusting in God. Many have become ministers.

Finally, here is another verse of reassurance I found helpful from **Jeremiah 29:11 (NIV):** *"For I know the plans I have for you,"* declares the LORD, *"plans to prosper you and not harm you, plans to give you hope and a future."* This is a promise from God to care for us if we would only look to Him and put our trust in Him. Speaking to many people in our church and from other walks of life, I constantly run into people who also have wonderful testimonies about the way God has helped them when they turned to Him for help, including miracles for some, and I know their stories are true through their sincerity. I often hear of new miracles occurring around the world, so God is still here to help us.

God's hand and presence has been there with me, even in the small, seemingly insignificant things, and so if He is there helping many other people at the same time, how mighty He must be.

The knowledge in my messages may be known by learned Christians; however, I have told my story and beliefs especially for those who are still in the wilderness and seeking answers to their needs, for those who need God, and for those lacking in faith. I have written this with piety and sincerity and in an understandable mode, for I feel many teachings these days are too complex for many, which is a pity. They may be interesting and well-spoken yet pass over the heads of many.

Of all the qualities we can acquire in our lives, the most important is love. God has shown this by example in Jesus and in the Bible. I know of its truth and reality, being deeply grateful to God for showing me His amazing love. I am not ashamed to talk

Conclusion

about it, as it is so important. It is also important to learn to love and respect oneself as God loves us before we can be truly loved by others. Love is the most important quality we can show one another. Unconditional, perfect love without conditions attached is by far the most important thing we can aspire to in our lives. It overcomes all, defeating hatred and fear, and will automatically pass on to other people to make our world a better place.

A few lessons I have learnt that work for a better life are the following; in putting love into practice, without ulterior motives for oneself, they really work. Give people a big sincere smile from the heart instead of a frown, and notice the results; it's amazing how it can cheer you and others up, and this is one form of effective love. We should challenge and change old attitudes and restrictive thought patterns; for example, remaining reserved, serious, and on guard when not necessary and keeping an open mind and heart to new, positive, cheerful ways. Be game and try laughing—it's good medicine—without making fun of others. Be patient, compassionate, thoughtful, kind, forgiving, polite, and generous; avoid arguing; and be helpful to others. Try not to judge or reject people for their appearance or ways as they may have a heart of gold despite having had a bad time, but encourage and show sincere faith in them, which may inspire and mean so much to them; the Lord will bless you for it. In this way, you will develop a spirit of freedom, joy, and happiness for the kindness you give to others will be returned to you. Put important verses from the Bible into your heart, and put them into practise. It may take time, learning, reading, and even Christian counseling to grow positively, but it does work, as God will help you, therefore it is well worth it. This is harder for those who unfortunately were not brought up with love, but it is worth pursuing as one's heart can be filled with love, especially after accepting Jesus as saviour. That is why it is so good to become involved with good, positive, cheerful, kind people, especially in a joyful church. Many Christians, including myself, believe it feels more personal when relating to God to call Him Father, so often you will hear Him called Father, or Father God.

My favourite verses from the Bible are these in **1 Corinthians 13:1–13 (NIV):** *"If I speak in the tongues of men and of angels, but have not love, I am only a resounding gong or a clanging cymbal. If I have the gift of prophecy and can fathom all mysteries and all knowledge, and if I have a faith that can move mountains, but have not love, I am nothing. If I give all I possess to the poor and surrender my body to the flames, but have not love, I gain nothing. Love is patient, love is kind. It does not envy, it does not boast, it is not proud. It is not rude, it is not self-seeking, it is not easily angered, it keeps no record of wrongs. Love does not delight in evil but rejoices with the truth. It always protects, always trusts, always hopes, always perseveres. Love never fails. But where there are prophecies, they will cease; where there are tongues, they will be stilled; where there is knowledge, it will pass away. For we know in part and we prophesy in part, but when perfection comes, the imperfect disappears. When I was a child, I talked like a child, I thought like a child, I reasoned like a child. When I became a man, I put childish ways behind me. Now we see but a poor reflection as in a mirror; then we shall see face to*

Conclusion

face. Now I know in part; then I shall know fully, even as I am fully known. And now these three remain: faith, hope and love. But the greatest of these is love."

Two remarkable experiences, surely from God, occurred when meditating on the final words for this book. Although I have now chosen a photo of Mount Cook for the front cover; when I processed the original front cover painting print for this book, (shown as a smaller print on the back cover), a small perfectly proportioned cross, like the one on which Jesus died, miraculously appeared in the peak of Mount Cook, with a small cup positioned exactly under the base of the cross (which may be difficult to see in the smaller print); and surely represents the cup by which we remember Jesus, and the blood He shed for us. It was not there before, and the cross is perfectly positioned over the top centre of the word God. This could not be by chance, or a coincidence. I did not place it there, and it is not obtrusive. That is another miracle, praise God—how truly amazing. Can one wonder why He placed it there? I am being touched by God again as I type these words.

Also when sitting in the patio having a cup of tea, looking up at the trees and praising God, thanking Him for His spiritual guidance in writing this true-life story, suddenly one of God's beautiful flying creations came and sat on a small branch next to me, as though for company, quite spiritual. Perhaps it symbolized Jesus saying, "Thank you for writing this book." What a wonderful ending. This is the only time this has ever happened. On my standing it came and hovered in front of my

face prior to leaving. Could this have been a coincidence? What a marvellous ending. "Oh thank-you Jesus."

My prayers are for you to realise the reality of our Father God's existence and His love for us all, through this book, that He will bless you always. So now, as Jesus said in part on the cross where He suffered and died to save us from eternal condemnation so that we may be reconciled back to God, in **John 19:30 (NIV):** *"It is finished."* This was the most important part of God's plan through His unconditional love for us, which I am so grateful to have experienced, and his amazing grace, yet there is much more, so read on in the New Testament to find more good news. Thank you for taking the time to read my story.

Bibliography

Victoria University of Wellington, Henderson, Jim. *4th and 6th Reserve Mechanical Transport Companies*, Retrieved from URLS: http://nzetc.victoria.ac.nz//tm/scholarly/name-022492.html, and index at, http://nzetc.victoria.ac.nz/tm/scholarly/tei-WH2Mech-N100027.html#name-028361-mention, Victoria University of Wellington. 2014.

Wikimedia Foundation Inc. 2014. Arctic Methane Release, Retrieved from URL: http://en.wikipedia.org/wiki/Arctic_methane_release. Also see Climate Change Science Program, http://en.wikipedia.org/wiki/Climate_Change_Science_Program

Romm, Joe. Climate Progress, 2013. Retrieved from URL: http://thinkprogress.org/climate/2013/10/02/2708911/fracking-ipcc-methane/

The Nationals. Senators and MPS from 1920. House of Representatives. Nock, Horace Keyworth, retrieved from URL: http://www.nationals.org.au/AboutTheNationals/OurHistory/

SenatorsandMPsfrom1920.aspx.The Nationals for Regional Australia, 2014.

Christians for Environmental Stewardship. "A Scriptural call for Environmental Stewardship", by Christians for Environmental Stewardship. Retrieved from URL: *http://www.christianecology. org/Stewardship.html*

Grey, John. The Revenge of Gaia, by James Lovelock. Retrieved from URL: *http://www.independent.co.uk/arts-entertainment/books/reviews/the-revenge-of-gaia-by-james-lovelock-524635.html*. independent.co.uk 2006

Scarlett2. Real Spiritual Experiences. Retrieved from URL: *http://www.spiritual-experiences.com/real-spiritual-story. php?story=898*. Spiritual-Experiences.com. 2011.

Endnote

The writer himself painted a picture of Mount Cook shown on the front cover of this book, from a similar position as the photo in the previous edition. He felt that Mount Cook itself often appears very spiritual. Painting pictures, like music, can relay joy and messages to us and are one of God's ways of communicating through us by showing others the beauty or darkness in many aspects of our lives. Paintings can add variety and enjoyment to our environment, just as nature can. Our lives comprise those of joys, aspirations, sorrows, problems, growth, and spiritual intervention, perhaps all depicted in this mountain painting by various degrees of colour, texture, tone, shadow, darkness and light, and finally, rising out of the darkness (or difficulties) into the light, being enlightened, knowing God and His love. John moved from New Zealand to Australia with his family at the age of ten and pursued a career in horticulture after receiving a Diploma of Horticulture. He worked as an Assistant

Superintendent and Technical Officer, working in Research with the CSIRO and running a plant nursery and orchard for ten years. He is an accomplished, successful artist with a Diploma of Commercial Art and a Certificate in Oil and Watercolour Painting, and he has won a number of prizes. John enjoys doing commission paintings for people. He will be embarking on a commission depicting *Jesus with desperate people reaching out to him*. This was a vision God had given a fellow church member, who told John that God desired this vision expressed on canvases. If you are interested in prints of these, you can inquire approximately 7-12 months after the publishing date of this book. If you would like more information about or would like to see these, you can write to John at **moret9lives@gmail.com**, where you can commission other work with him, as he paints various subjects. A well-known artist taught him, so John has been a successful artist-painter for most of his life and has sold many paintings.

www.ingramcontent.com/pod-product-compliance
Lightning Source LLC
Chambersburg PA
CBHW051429290426
44109CB00016B/1488